BEAR

Baiting & Trapping Black Bear

by
Richard E. Faler, Jr.

A Beaver Pond Publication

Greenville, Pennsylvania

BEAR—*Baiting & Trapping Black Bear*
©1993 Richard E. Faler, Jr.

All drawings and cover sketch by Bob Noonan

Photos on pages 23, 85 and 89
provided by Richard P. Smith

Photos on pages 30 and 41 provided by
Maine Department of Inland Fisheries & Wildlife

All other photos by Richard E. Faler, Jr.

Beaver Pond Publishing
P.O. Box 224, Greenville, PA 16125
Phone: (724) 588-3492 • Fax: (724) 588-2486
Email: beaverpond@pathway.net or help@bookblender.com
website: beaverpondpublishing.com or bookblender.com

Table of Contents

As a small token of my gratitude, I wish to dedicate these pages to the Maine men who introduced me to the rich outdoor heritage of that state. My sincere thanks goes to Joe Baldwin, Art Bousquet, Bob Noonan and the Day clan—Jim, Gary and Mark.

INTRODUCTION

U nder the watchful eyes of Mount Katahdin and the twin peaks of the Spencer Mountains rolls a land of rich heritage. Here, timber reigns king, the moose has become the unwitting, awkward aristocrat, and the Atlantic salmon beckons to the sophisticate. In the land called Maine, everything of importance spawns from the outdoors. One cannot divorce himself from its tradition and history.

One can hunt moose in Maine. One can watch a grilse or mature salmon roll as it takes a Jock Scott. One can hunt the partridge — or simply enjoy the local accent as a native talks about a trip above the Golden Road to pot a few for Thanksgiving dinner. These all paint a picture of the outdoor lure of Maine.

No season in Maine matches fall. Here is the harvest time for the hunter and trapper. As the saplings crowding the beaver bogs turn a fiery red, the moose and whitetails rub the last snakeskins of velvet off their antlers. The outdoorsmen begin their treks into the countryside to partake of the ritual of the hunt. It is a time of excitement and electricity. The fresh frost, crisp air and whipping wind clear the mind and the soul. As the leaves brown and drop, one can trap for elusive fisher along the hardwood/evergreen edges. He can try to capture the nomadic, mostly aquatic, otter. Blanket beaver can be pursued in the bogs or the clever coyote along the logging two-tracks. All are a challenge. But none, in my estimation, are as uniquely the property of the Pine Tree State as the challenge of trapping the black bear.

A trapper might be able, if he is a government trapper or has a nuisance permit, to trap the black bear for nuisance control, for live transfer, or for study. A biologist or nuisance control agent in Alaska might match wits with grizzly. An Afrikaner may find his quarry to be a leopard. For the sportsman without any special government or scientific authority, however, the black bear is the largest possible catch — and only in Maine. No other state or country, to my knowledge, provides for a legal capture of the black bear, or anything larger, under an easy-to-obtain trapping permit. The black bear, then, is truly the big game quarry of the sport trapper.

The reason for writing *BEAR: Baiting and Trapping Black Bear* is three-fold. The main reason, even though it might not be evident in the reading, is to preserve this bit of New England State heritage.

Too many obscure or unpublicized traditions are being lost. Outdoor pursuits are no exception. It would be a shame to ever lose this part of our world through it not being properly recorded.

Secondly, though this is primarily a how-to-do book, it is my desire to have part of the aroma of the Maine outdoors intrigue and endear more folks. A book on bear trapping must surely offer the scent.

Finally, the most obvious reason for this book — to show how one can trap a bear. And in conjunction with this and just as critical for success, how to bait a bear.

Bear baits are almost a science unto themselves. They are an integral part of both the successful bear trapper and of the hunter who wishes to hunt a bear by sitting over a bait. In this sense, then, this book should have value to both bear trappers and hunters.

I do not presume to be a great bear trapper. My experience is necessarily limited by my living 800 miles from Maine. If I was a Maine boy, I'd trap a bear each season. Distance and other considerations do not allow this.

My experience and that of a friend (from Pennsylvania, also) who trekked to this state to successfully take a bruin were the beginnings of this work. My acquaintance and communication with three Maine trappers who have taken quite a number of bear have brought this to a completion. I trust this book will offer something to all who read its pages — whether the curious, the beginning bear trapper, or an old-timer at the pursuit.

Whatever your purpose, good luck and enjoy the pursuit of the bear trapper in the land of bogs and brooks, the firs and the poplar.

EQUIPMENT

THE FOOT-GRIPPER

The bear trap typically seen on mantels in motels and bars is the huge 16" jawspread grizzly bear trap. The usual jawspread on black bear foot-gripping traps is 9". (Jawspread is the widest point between the two jaws after the trap is set and the jaws are flat on the ground.)

When one says "bear trapping," visions of huge, toothed traps pop up. For the record, all steel-jawed bear traps are now antiques and are no longer manufactured. Even here, the average person thinks of the largest ever steel-jawed traps used. These were designed for grizzly bear and were the Newhouse #6 with a jaw spread of 16". This trap is NOT a black bear trap.

A number of black bear traps have been manufactured in past decades. These follow the popular longspring style of traps, a type still manufactured in much smaller sizes for efficient capture of everything from weasel to wolverine. A popular brand in its heyday, the Newhouse line of traps included three styles for bear: Newhouse #50 (9" jaw spread), Newhouse #150 (9" jaw spread), and Newhouse #5 ($11^3/_4$" jaw spread).

These traps have two springs of folded metal (long springs) on either end of a set of jaws. A trigger device holds the jaws open. When the bear steps on the trap pan (a small flat piece of metal in the center of the jaws that attaches to the trigger), the trigger releases and the jaws close.

Setting this trap for black bear brings back the fullest experience for the trapper — in one sense. Yet, it also brings one back to reality. True, an antique steel-jawed trap will certainly clamp a bear. It is also a dangerous device to handle. Because of this, the Maine Fish and Wildlife Department has extra regulations for setting this trap. These follow:

It is unlawful to set a bear trap unless it is enclosed by 2 strands of wire, one 2 and one 4 feet from the ground. The wire must be held securely in position not less than 5 yards nor more than 10 yards from the enclosed trap.

The enclosure must be marked with signs bearing the words "BEAR TRAP" in letters at least 3 inches in height, and the signs must be spaced around the enclosure, securely attached to the top strand of wire, at intervals of not more than 20 feet. (Note: These provisions do not apply if cable traps are used.)

These special requirements are the minimum for the safety of other humans when setting such large traps. Unfortunately, it also means that very expensive antiques are left in the woods with signs pointing to their location. Theft can be as likely as a bear when the set is visited.

Few folks now set these large traps for bear, even in Maine. Many of the resident trappers I talked with felt the cost and the risk these traps required weren't worth it. I would have to agree. These traps are a valid method for a purist "mountain man" to try. Because of the above mentioned factors, however, I do not recommend them.

THE FOOT-SNARE

To my knowledge, there are two foot-snare traps produced. These are the Aldrich and Mowatt. I've used the Aldrich. It is probably the most commonly used of the two. Both foot-traps incorporate a spring/trigger assembly which fires a loop up and around a bear's leg. It invariably becomes tightened around the ankle or even the toes.

The foot-snare has been a godsend in many ways. In practical terms, it meets the requirements of a perfect trap. Compared to other

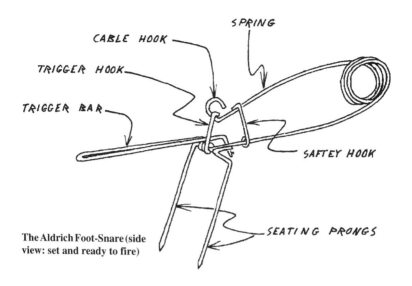

CABLE HOOK

TRIGGER HOOK

TRIGGER BAR

SPRING

SAFTEY HOOK

SEATING PRONGS

The Aldrich Foot-Snare (side view: set and ready to fire)

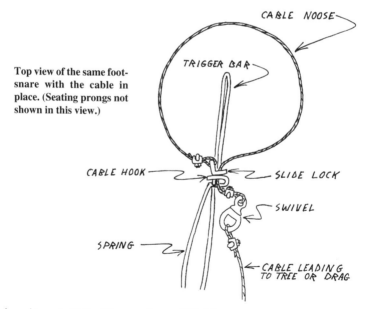

CABLE NOOSE

Top view of the same foot-snare with the cable in place. (Seating prongs not shown in this view.)

TRIGGER BAR

CABLE HOOK

SLIDE LOCK

SWIVEL

SPRING

CABLE LEADING TO TREE OR DRAG

devices it costs little. Figure about $30.00 each. It weighs little and is compact. For the trapper, whether sport, government or biologist, it is, very importantly, effective. It is not dangerous, is easy to set, and rarely harms the bear in any long-term or permanent manner. Biologists country-wide use this trap for studying of the black bear. The bears are often trapped, tranquilized, tagged after data collection, and released with no aftereffects. One such Maine biologist is responsible for more than 800 bear captures. The foot-snare is truly the ideal device for the bear trapper.

An added bonus comes from the game regulations. Unlike the steel-jawed traps, the warning signs and fencing wires are not required. This minimizes the work at the set and the likelihood of another person finding the set. The less a trapper advertises his whereabouts to others, the less his sets will be disturbed. An undisturbed set will usually take more game.

The foot-snare should be the number one choice for anyone outfitting for a bear trip.

THE NECK SNARE

Neck snares are very effective for bear. They are a loop of cable with a locking device, much like a foot-snare, only they use no trigger or spring. They are suspended so a bear puts his head through the loop. As the bear walks on, the loop snugs down, locks and kills the bear.

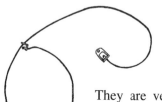

The black bear is easy to snare. He quickly succumbs to the snare with relatively little fighting. Like the foot-snares, the neck snares cost little, weigh almost nothing, and are easy to use. They are very effective. They also kill the bear making it a tool to be used only when a dead bear is the goal.

IMPORTANT: The neck snare is illegal in Maine. It is a tool used by nuisance control trappers only. It will be covered in this book as a comparison, and as a guide for those in other states and provinces who wish to try them for control work.

CABLE AND CONNECTIONS

Since the fur boom of the late '70s and early '80s, more fine-tuning of trapping equipment has taken place than in the previous history of trapping. This has spilled over to an extent in bear trapping.

Fine-tuning of equipment advertises a careful, conscientious trapper. Traps of any kind straight from the box can take fur. Fine-tuning, however, gives a greater edge to the trapper. It allows for the trap to trigger when the animal is in the best possible position for a solid capture. It also means that once the animal is grasped, it will be held in the most humane and effective manner to minimize escapes.

Most of the fine-tuning of the foot-snare takes place in how the set is constructed and how the anchoring is done. The set construction is covered later.

The first adjustment to the foot-snare ensures no deer or small game will become accidentally caught in the loop. The Maine game law reads: *Cable traps with a closing diameter of not less than 2¹/₂" may be used in trapping bear.* It only takes a few minutes to meet this requirement. Close down the loop so it is slightly greater than the legal minimum. Hold the cable where the sliding lock is resting.

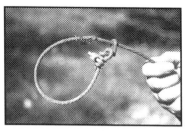

A tight wrapping of wire creates a "deer-stop" which prevents the loop from closing too small. This keeps deer and small game from becoming caught.

Holding that spot on the cable, open the loop some so you have room to work. Now take a stiff wire, maybe a 16 or 14 gauge, and wrap it tightly on the spot you are holding. Wrap several windings of wire. Now take a pair of pliers and twist the wire ends so everything is tight and won't slip. This is called a "stop," obviously because it stops the lock from sliding further.

A ³/₁₆" diameter extension cable comes attached to the Aldrich foot-snare. Its 5¹/₂ foot length fits most anchoring situations.

I remember one successful set where the bear trail meandered through a boggy tangle. In a relatively open location in that claustraphobic spruce stand, the trail passed within five feet of a straight-up spruce. Though the trunk of the spruce was too far for the cable to wrap around and clamp, the trail here was perfect. Two of the spruce's far-reaching roots snaked through the thick moss beyond the bear trail. Where the trail crossed the roots, they formed natural stepping sticks, forcing the bear to reach over them and place his paw in the same exact spot each time he traveled through. One doesn't pass up such sure-bets and takes extra effort to utilize them.

I dug in a trail set between the two roots. Since no tree was close enough to use the stock extension cable, the cable was worked and threaded under a rather large root of the same spruce. It was no flimsy root, either. Not perfectly round, it was approximately eight inches in diameter. This set securely held a bear that dressed approximately 130 pounds — about average for a Maine black. While the spruce was rather scarred and chewed, the root was intact and in excellent shape.

That's the best way to use the foot-snare — anchor it with the extension cable it comes equipped with, and forget additional extensions.

Sometimes the situation demands a longer reach to securely anchor the trap. You can go one of two ways: cable or chain. A log chain can be bolted around a tree, then clamped to the extension cable. A bear-sized chain, not to be confused with the 2/0 and 3/0 coyote trap chain, needs to be of quite a heft. If there's a weak link the bear will surely find it. Chain in the proper size to ensure holding the largest bruin will take quite a mountain man to pack in. I wouldn't use any chain for bear unless it had welded links. Such a chain costs.

The absolute best means of achieving extra length with the tie-down is with extra cable of that same $^3/_{16}$" diameter.

Let's compare the cable and chain. Cable of $^3/_{16}$" diameter (use uncoated cable) has a breaking strength of approximately 840 pounds. At the time of this writing, from a local supplier, the cable cost 29 cents a foot. Welded link chain of $^3/_{16}$" ($^3/_{16}$" is the diameter of the steel which is made into the links) has a breaking strength of approximately 750 pounds — almost 100 pounds less than the cable. This chain costs 80 cents a foot. Would you rather spend almost three times as much for a product that is harder to use, weighs too much to be practical, and has less strength? The answer here is to save your money and use cable.

Always carry at least one extra snare cable. A miss or an escape can kink up the snare portion of the foot-snare. Having an extra snare cable on you will save a lot of time and ensure a well-made set. It takes ten minutes to loosen the cable clamps holding the original snare in place and tightening on the new. Along with this extra snare cable, carry a five foot and a ten foot piece for anchoring extensions. Every anchoring possibility can be taken care of with these pieces.

To ease the carrying, even if you place them in a packbasket, coil

Installing two cable clamps side-by-side and facing in opposite directions is good insurance against cable slipping at the wrong, critical moment.

the cable. Take a light wire, or even tape, and tie the coils so they don't spring open. The cut cable ends can snag clothing and cut fingers. It's extra work, but you might want to wrap two or three turns of electrician's tape on each end to cover the cut wires. The end wraps can be removed before use at the set.

The fox and coyote trapper has stakes for anchoring, four-coil kits to add spring power, auxiliary swivels, attachments for cross staking, pan covers, Underalls and Trapper's Caps to keep the dirt from under the pan, and on and on. The bear trapper has ... cable clamps.

The serious bear trapper, and every bear trapper should be very serious in this pursuit, needs to carry a pocket full of extra cable clamps. Clamps hold everything together. They keep the ripping, tugging, powering, jerking boar black bear at the set. The clamps, though small, do a big job. Their importance cannot be overlooked.

The first thing to do on a foot-snare is to tighten all the manufacturer-installed clamps. Most will be A-OK. To be on the safe side, you must double check them. Next, double check every clamp you install. Whether pre-season or at the set, never move on to another clamp without the insurance of making certain both nuts on each clamp are very tight and secure. Lose that big bruin because of a loose clamp and you'll kick yourself black-and-blue.

When attaching extension cables or when attaching the cable to an anchor or drag, use two cable clamps side-by-side. It's also a good practice to add a second at each spot where the factory has one installed. When placing the second in position, turn it so it faces the opposite direction of the first. In other words, have the two-nut end of one clamp facing the same direction as the U-shaped back of the second. Only a .30 caliber slug will anchor a bear more securely than cable clamped in this manner. The second clamp is insurance. Having it face the opposite direction fine-tunes against the long odds of a really rambunctious bear having the cable next to the clamp's smooth side from slipping. It probably won't happen — but if the biologists taking many hundreds of bear have had it happen a few times, why risk your trophy being one of those long shots? Don't. Use two clamps and face them oppositely.

MISCELLANEOUS EQUIPMENT AND ADJUSTMENT

Keeping to the traditional look and feel of the old-time trappers, all a bear trapper's gear, except for bait, can be carried in a large packbasket. Personal tastes come into play here, but few hunting coats can hold everything (foot-snare spring assemblies and cables, extra cable, shovel, and axe and/or pruning saw for the big items). With a bucket of bait being taken in at each set, unless a partner accompanies, there'll not be enough hands to carry everything.

Five-gallon plastic buckets hold and carry the messiest concoctions of bear baits. A half a dozen of these will outfit a lone bear trapper's camp. Metal ones certainly work, but the plastic are easier to come by and don't make so much noise.

A heavy-duty trapper's trowel or a small spade must be a part of the trapper's outfit. Bait holes and trap beds require more digging than mere fingernails can stand. Heavy-duty is the key word. Whimpy, five-and-dime garden trowels waste your money. Buy a shovel or large trowel with some heft. Digging next to a bog or on a mountain finds one colliding with all kinds of rocks and roots. Prying and whacking, while not the recommended use of any trowel or shovel, are an inherent part of digging at a bear set.

All those cable clamps make carrying a wrench mandatory. A rachet and appropriate-sized socket are quicker and easier to use. Whichever you use, carrying a spare in your pocket or back in the truck is only common sense.

Though additional equipment, I like to carry a pair of heavy hand pruners. They help me to remove thumb-sized roots in trap beds with half the grunting of shredding them off with the trapper's trowel. They double up in snipping off brush and pencil-sized branches for set making. Hand pruners aren't a must, but they are handy.

Along with all those cable clamps, a bear trapper would look pretty silly without a means to tighten and loosen the nuts. A rachet and proper-sized socket make the work quick and efficient.

A deep socket is best. If you won't or can't get anything but a regular-depth socket, here's a trick that might come in handy. When tightening the clamp nuts, the screw-part of the clamp might be too long and keep a shallow socket from fitting down over the nut. In other words, you screw on the nut so far and then it's too far down the threads to allow the socket to seat far enough to turn the nut any further. In this situation remove the socket from the rachet. Place the socket down over the nut. Now slip the rachet into the socket, but not far enough to lock it on. You can gain a quarter inch or so additional tightening depth this way.

With the immense strength of a black bear and the importance of securely tightened clamps, I'd shy away from jury-rigged tightening techniques. It'd be far better to simply spend a few bucks and get that deeper socket.

A good practice is to carry a box and open end wrench in a pocket — in addition to the rachet and socket. This is a back-up tool in case something happens to the rachet and socket — things have a way of breaking or getting lost when they are critical components to the task at hand.

An axe, pruning saw or bow saw find their main use in making cubby sets or in cutting drags. Green wood can be cut more efficiently and with much less danger with a sharp saw. Regardless, the axe or saw need only be carried to the trap site during the initial set up. After that, they can be forgotten and left in the vehicle. They'll then get more use removing blowdowns that block the back roadways.

A rifle or revolver becomes very important when checking sets. The goal of all the activities in this book is to bag a bear. It'll take a slug of metal to finish the job. A trapped bear can seem docile, almost tame. The power and rage under that black coat can, like a light switch, come boiling out of every pore in an instant. Caution is always advised.

I've shot a black bear between the eyes with a .22 magnum rimfire. That small pill of lead cured all the ills of that particular bruin. Yet, it was a very controlled situation and I had the necessary luxury of taking my time with the aim. Many black bear have been dropped under similar circumstances with a small .22 bullet ... I did have a .30-30 close by—in case.

The trouble with .22 rimfires on black bear are the loads' lack of shocking power and tissue damage. Unless the first shot nails the bear just so, there's going to be trouble. A wounded bear, even a fatally wounded one, will dissolve a box of .22 rimfire bullets in its surge of adrenaline.

Take a .30 caliber, high-power backup if you want to drop a bear with a .22 rimfire. Better yet, so you don't lose a hard-earned trophy or something a little more personal and precious, begin with the .30 caliber. Drop the bear quick and certain.

A downed bear instantly requires a knife for gutting. Whether a sheath or folding model, sharpness of blade counts. It's better to dress game with a fresh razor blade than with an eight-inch blade on which you can bare-butt ride to town. A four- to six-inch blade that's kept to a fine edge will make the dressing and skinning job as simple as it gets.

In Maine the steel foot-grippers and the foot-snares both need the user's name and address attached. Metal trap tags are usually used. For foot-snares, wire them to the extension cable next to the swivel, then roll the tag itself around the cable. For steel traps, wire them to the trap chain. Metal trap tags can be ordered from a number of trapline suppliers. See the listing at the end of this book.

Odd accessories such as string or plastic bags may be needed for various baiting techniques. Outfit these according to the baiting methods to be used.

Most land trappers (those after non-aquatic furbearers like coyote and fox) take great pains to dye their traps in a wood solution. This prevents rust and kills unnatural odors. These same trappers wear gloves and boots, and take every possible precaution to keep human odor from the set site. The purpose is to leave nothing behind which may cause the furbearer to hesistate or to become alarmed. These efforts will rarely help a bear trapper.

Because bear baits by their very nature have a lot of human scent around them, the bear expect it. They don't get all panicky when they whiff some human odor — as long as it isn't hot, fresh- from-the-body molecules. The scent leaching off your body can spook them. The lingering odor on the ground usually won't. For this reason, you need not wear gloves or otherwise worry about leaving your scent on the trap or at the set.

BAITING

Carrying out a bear is tough work. A lot of bear require the efforts of several to drag them out. Before the celebrations and the hauling, though, you have to bag the critter. The first step (the most critical) is finding the food sources and then getting baits hit on a regular basis by at least one bruin.

Joe Baldwin led me to my first successful bear trapping venture. Joe, of Garland, Maine, makes his living as a professional outdoorsman. Joe actively traps furbearers for the pelts. As a guide, he also makes sure the visiting outdoorsman has a decent chance for a successful hunting or fishing trip—and, in my case, for trapping.

Joe has been in on approximately 100 bear kills. I depended a lot on his knowledge on my first bear trapping trip to Maine. I feel his knowledge has a solid base that will stand the test.

I asked Joe, *"What do you consider the most important part of bear trapping?"*

He instantly replied, *"Probably advance preparation. The advance work of finding the bear, the bear that you want to trap, and then really baiting him up in good shape to establish travelways. Then you can blind trap him coming into the bait."*

That advance preparation, primarily baiting, has been echoed by every other successful bear trapper I've ever talked with. Baiting in advance guarantees nothing, but it comes closer to handing a trapper a sure-bet than anything else that can be done.

Cold rolling can work for black bear. Unlike the catches a cold-rolling coyote or marten trapper can realize, the cold-rolling bear trapper will find a lot of empty mornings on the trapline. Cold roll if you must, but keep in mind that advance work on baiting the bear will give an awesome return for the effort.

For a Maine resident, advance work requires only a little time. Non-residents face a dilemma that's a function of time and money. For the best advance work, non-residents must take a lot of extra vacation time to run baits or hire a man-on-the-spot, a guide, to do it for him. For most folks, renting hot baits from a guide or outfitter is the most economical in both time and money.

For the trapper who does the entire shabang himself, he must work out a baiting system. The first step is to find probable locations for the baits.

Good trapping cannot be equated to a simplistic sum of "taking fur." Behind that "taking fur" lies a person who has learned more about the furbearer, his habits and habitat than many (I didn't say "most") wildlife biologists. I mean no disrespect here. While the biologists often study a broad range of creatures in different capacities, the best trappers have spent a lifetime studying one or two species, developing an almost empathetic sixth sense concerning that one or two species.

I wallow in the superficially naive statement of master trapper Charlie Dobbins of Canton, Ohio, who proclaims: *"Let the animal tell you"*. Charlie has made this statement countless times, to me privately and to the trapping fraternity in his many books and articles. Charlie traps at a level of excellence few can ever dream of attaining. His simple *"let the animal tell you"* has a commonsense meaning loaded with all the sage advice carried by the three wise men of the Orient.

When Charlie sees mink acting consistently under a certain set of environmental conditions, he traps them accordingly. If the behavior is alien to what is written in the textbooks and trapping booklets, so what? Charlie lets the mink tell him what the mink will do in each situation.

A successful bear trapper, or hunter for that matter, must do likewise. If looking for bear, let the bear himself tell you where he'll be and what he'll do. As accurate and all encompassing as I am trying to make this book, if the bear in a certain season and location demand a totally different approach, then follow the bear's lead and forget this book.

Too many folks figure that they can throw bait out anywhere and the bear will find it. Wrong. The bear might find a percentage of such baits. Haphazardly baiting miles of real estate, even in prime bear country, will find a lot of untouched bait rotting and enough boot leather to build a new cow being worn away for naught. You need to target the baits for maximum results.

Most furbearer trapping orients around structure. Coyotes move through saddles and passes. Bobcat wander sandy, palmetto ridges overlooking Southeast rivers. Fox gravitate toward the high mounds in the pastures. Otter, beaver, mink and muskrat follow the waterways. Many traplines, both prescouted and cold-rolling, have each set placed according to structure that will funnel or attract the targeted furbearer.

Bear will certainly travel through saddles and follow ridges. The best trappers and the best bait hunters, though, know the way to a bear: through his stomach. Just as placed baits will draw a bear to the trapper's snare or hunter's projectile, the natural food supply will show where to place the baits to begin with.

Rarely does the black bear go hungry. He feeds on an infinitely wide variety of fruits, nuts, small animals, fresh carcasses, honey comb, and, yes, man's garbage. While being adaptable in feeding habits, he likes variety. As the long, cold snows of Maine's winter float ever closer, the prehibernating bear takes advantage of every bumper crop he can. His body demands a thick layer of fat before that annual sleep and his stomach must be kept full to produce that layer. In this tunnel-visioned purpose, the black bear will follow Mother Nature's succession of ripening crops.

In the late summer, berries provide a big cash crop for the ravenous bear. The raspberries fade to blackberries. As the blackberries filter down, by the first week of September, the corn is in milk and the bear move in in force. Bear can be devastating to a small cornfield, knocking down and destroying large patches each night. The corn hardens and is harvested while the nuts become accessible by dropping to the ground. Apples ripen then, too, and are good until late October and early November.

A transient trapper may have difficulty following the food sources. He won't know where the old grown-up orchards flourish or where the biggest concentrations of nut trees cluster. The raspberries, five to six foot high acres of them, grow up in the clearcuts. Unfortunately, though easy to find, they are pretty well done for during the time when a non-resident would be trying to locate and bait bear.

To find black bear, get in touch with the current food source (wild cherries, here). *(Richard P. Smith)*

Taking the first logical step in honing in on the current food source, check with the local folks, including the game warden, and this general information should be easy to find. Hear *"Yep, there's a pile of apples this year."* and you'll know that this will make up one of the major types of food to locate. Have a warden exclaim *"Them bear are just cleaning up on the beech."* and you'll know to keep an eye out for beech ridges.

Once the food *du jour* is identified, combine any leads from the locals with gasoline and foot power to try to find concentrations of the food — and of the bear.

Particularly in cornfields, it may be possible to find a regularly used bear trails around the edges. If so, if the season is already in, then you've got an instant hot set location. If you're doing preseason work, then set up a bait nearby and keep it going until the actual trapping begins.

While Joe Baldwin generally believes the average Maine bear has a territory of somewhere around 25 square miles, he also feels they will travel some to abundant food sources. For example, when the corn milks, he feels that some of the bear resident of the Joe-Mary lake country move down to his Garland vicinity to feed. The corn represents a banquet that'll really put on the bear fat. Joe feels it will

Apples are common in much of the Maine countryside and are a big draw for bear. Finding a concentration of food, such as a cornfield next to an old orchard, is the first step in getting in touch with a bear.

draw the Joe-Mary bear over 40-some miles of terrain.

Keep this in mind when trapping. Bumper crops of bear feed will pull the bear a distance to your baits. It will also pull the bear away if you do not have the baits placed in the general area of those current food sources.

The ideal bear baiting situation is to set up baits close to the major food sources. This cannot always be done. Sometimes you'll have out more baits than food source locations. Arithmetic tells you that some baits will not be next to the food currently being scarfed up by the bear. Also, if baiting for a while, the food sources may shift while you're still baiting and trapping. If a bear is coming to your bait and the food sources change, the bear, if the new food isn't too far, will still visit your bait on his rounds. Only if he moves a considerable distance will the bait go dead because he has changed his diet.

Certainly, as the apples ripen, place bait right next to or in an old, wild orchard. What if the bear are into the nuts? Well, look for large areas which have an extra large number of producing nut trees. Because the nut trees will be scattered, you won't have a definite spot, such as an orchard, to bait. But you will have general locations, such as a ridge or mountain side with an exception number of nut trees. Bait here, not on some mountain side that is 100% evergreen.

Bear will be found anywhere in bear country. Yet, while with Joe on-and-off over a five year period, I noticed a similarity with the baits he took me to. Sometimes I accompanied him and his bait buckets so we could try coyote calling at the bait sites. Other times it was so I could set foot-snares. At any rate, I never saw a bait high on a ridge. They were always close to a boggy spot, near water of some sort.

Joe begins baiting as soon as possible. That is now, the way the laws are set up, 30 days before the season begins. Even though bear trapping in the 1991 season began on October 1 (ending October 31), hunting over baits opened on September 2. One could legally set out bear baits August 3. (Check the regulations each year. The dates and other details can change from season to season.)

Since the baiting begins during the hottest part of the year, Joe takes this into account. Bear in the summer need a lot of wet holes to lay in to cool off. They like a wet area, whether it's a beaver flowage, stream or just a swamp. They're a lot like a pig in wanting to keep cool in the summer.

Combine a water source for keeping cool with a close food source so he doesn't have to travel 20 miles to feed and you'll have an excellent location to bait. Give the bear everything he wants in one spot and baiting him is easy. You've got to make it convenient for him and bait right in his living room.

Don't get paranoid about finding a big mountain of bear food before setting your bait out. As in all types of trapping, hunting and fishing, you need the basic rules to guide you, but you must also be flexible and adaptive. If the particular region you choose to bait and trap has no cornfields and no apple orchards for a good 50 miles in any direction, then they certainly won't be a consideration in locating the bear. If such in-season food sources are in the area, though, that's the most likely area to find the bear. And that cornfield or apple orchard close to a beaver bog will probably be the living room of at least one bear.

Once the general places to bait have been picked, either by seeing bear sign, finding an area with the timely food source, or by guess and by gosh, the specific site must be determined. Baits to be used by hunters require the most thought.

A bait to be hunted must have easy access. That doesn't mean you just step out of the truck and begin watching the bait. It means that the hunter can get to the bait quietly. Bear may be investigating or feeding on a bait at any hour. You don't want to spook him off by a noisy approach. Many hunters would spook a bear if the access trail was lined with several feet of goose down. Nothing will help this kind of person. For the average person taking care in what he does and taking his time in doing it, a bear can be moved in on without spooking him. In order for this to happen, the trail the hunter follows to the bait should have quiet footing. Six inches of crispy, crunchy leaves allow no winning on the hunter's corner. But a trail over ankle deep moss? Super!

The access trail should have a corridor free of branches high enough so there isn't a constant swishing of branches as they glide over the hunting coat. A little detour here or there, though adding ten minutes and 30 yards to the bait stalk, may transform exercise into a real hunt. One trip to the bait when it's first set up can make the access noiseless — just snap or cut off the offending branches and saplings. A hunter doesn't need a super highway. Ducking under a log or slithering sideways around brush is part of the experience but a bad spot of noisy travel can be doctored up to help the hunter get the drop on the bruin.

Whether the trail in can be rendered soft of sound or not, the bait site must take two factors into consideration.

The first is the wind. The predominant wind direction should waft the hunter's stench away from the bait and the bear's expected line of travel. A secondary stand for oddball wind direction also needs constructed. Of course, most bowhunters and many gun hunters will use tree stands from which to wait for their chance. Wind decreases in importance as the waiting hunter rises in elevation. Make certain the tree stand is solid and safe, and doesn't make any squeaking noises.

The second consideration at a hunter's bait demands a stand, or stands, which allow a clear view of the bait. If the hunter has no chance of taking a clear shot at the quarry, everything has been for naught. This doesn't mean the bait is in the middle of an open field. Even hunter baits should be in secluded cover.

These considerations, so critical when baiting for a hunter, become mental exercises for the bait to be trapped. The trap does its work during the trapper's absence. Noiseless access, wind direction, and clear shooting lanes do not affect the trapper. They cannot be a problem when the trapper is off checking other baits or is back in camp at night sleeping.

The trap site can be a real close place. Since no shooting lanes from the ground or a tree stand are needed, you can bait any location that promises bear. I'd opt to bait the thicker locations on purpose. They give the bear a better feeling of security. For the trapper, thicker locations seem to produce better bear trails to the bait. Wherever the trail snakes through the brush and deadfalls, you'll have an ideal location for a trail set. The brush, in addition to the bear's habit, will combine to funnel his foot right into the trap.

I trapped two different baits, maybe 40 miles apart, the first year I trapped black bear. By driving carefully, we could take the family van on a two-track to within 200 to 300 yards of the bait. The second bait could only be approached by vehicle to within 500 yards or so. As in all trapping, go as far as you have to from the vehicle to get to the hot spot, the ideal spot — but go no further. Don't waste time taking that daily rebaiting and trap checking walk if a shorter distance will get the job done. But, if 100 yards closer to the parking spot is second best in location, then go the extra yards. And if you get that not-so-common, 300-pounder? You'll wish you'd gotten him closer. And if you get the average 120-pounder? You'll think him 300 by the time you get him dragged back to the truck.

One last item on specific site. To a bear trapper, Maine seems to be a big rock and boulder field with a skin of moss and trees. A lot of areas have good soil (between the rocks) and bunches of sand. When digging a trap bed, though, you can begin to dig hole after hole on excellent trails, trails through lowland bogs, and hit boulder after boulder. In some spots, it is almost impossible to punch a hole deep enough for even a mediocre set. It's not practical to check what's under the soil around a bait anywhere a bear may begin packing down a trail. Take a look around when deciding on where to bait, not just for bear possibilities, but for geological base. If you look to the left and right of a small low spot possibility, and see a sheet of solid rock coming toward you from the left and another moving in from the right, you might have nothing under the leaf debris and moss but a slab of granite. If that's what you see, check it out. You might want to move on. There are a lot of potential bait sites in Maine that are only half rock. Don't waste sweat baiting bedrock you won't be able to sink a hole into.

BAIT

Bear eat anything. They do.

The guides and trappers could give a flip. They want maximum results. They don't want to lay out a bait that the bear will eat, but indifferently. They want to draw the bear in and keep him coming.

Some trappers bait bear with hot pig guts — the stunk-up innards from butchered hogs. This works. They also use fish. This works. They are not the ideal.

In all critters, certain baits and smells seem to excel. Beaver trappers from Alaska to Alabama know that quaking aspen, popple or poplar, whatever you want to call it, is the strawberry shortcake bait for trapping beaver. No other bait will bring in the flattails like this light-barked tree. Likewise, castor, the scent a beaver secretes, draws them in like no other odor.

For bear there is strawberry shortcake bait and odor. The universally best baits are pastries and fresh beef. The unanimous choice of attracting odors is anise, the licorice smell.

The pastries bring out the bruin's sweet tooth. Most bakery shops and bread chains sell day-old donuts and sweet rolls at a greatly reduced price. Such a secret weapon these are! Joe Baldwin, for example, uses dozens upon dozens of creme horns, a filled crust-type pastry, for his baiting and bear trapping. They'll walk a bear right into your snare-loop.

Keeping in line with the "Yogi the Bear" sweet tooth syndrome, honey and molasses can be lumped with the pastries. Honey and molasses are both often used like icing on the bait. They add the little extra ompf — the high octane on the bait to keep it running at peak efficiency.

Honey and molasses can be purchased through normal channels. Both Art Bousquet, a Maine trapper I met while trapping in the Florida Panhandle, and Joe Baldwin use cattle grain or horse feed as part of their baiting strategy. These feeds have molasses added to them at the grist mill. Livestock feeds, then, are an offering to Yogi's sweet tooth.

Beef, the number one meat bait, certainly costs more than pastry. It's not too bad though when you get away from sirloin and finagle buckets of bones and scraps from butcher shops.

A meat that is on par with beef is beaver. Beaver trappers eat it and feel they are chowing down a feast. The bear feel likewise. Since bear trappers normally trap other critters in their respective seasons, entire beaver carcasses are frozen after pelting and saved for the next fall's bear season. For the man with a big freezer and the staying power to buy his supper instead of eating his bear bait, beaver are an excellent choice when beef scraps cannot be had or will cost too much.

We often hear of fish as bear bait. Photos and stories of the grizzly and brown bear of the Northwest slapping and munching spawning salmon surely feed the fish bait rumors. In reality, fish are one

Black bear have a super sweet tooth. Their love of honey is well documented and they will destroy a bee tree when they are lucky enough to find one in order to harvest the honey. Honey, molasses and other sweets are powerful attractants to the bear bait.

of the worst bear baits. They will draw bear, to be sure. The problem with fish is they disintegrate so rapidly. Their progression from fresh flesh to putrid tissue to disintegrated nothing is like melting hailstones on a summer day. Now you see them, now you don't. I've used fish baits for decades for coon and mink trapping, and this bait must constantly be replenished or replaced.

Fish also draw an excess amount of small game. Feeding skunk and having raccoon trip the foot-snares won't help you trap a bear. At least this state has the good graces to have fenced off the opossum — the more southerly and westerly scourge of bait sets. Opossum are completely protected in Maine, but probably not a hundred call the Pine Tree State home.

The licorice smell of anise wrinkles the bear's black nose in fits of desire. It is *the* scent to use while baiting. The best baits, fresh beef and sweets, don't have the power of odor to travel the breezes for but a few yards. Anise flexes its biceps and strong-arms bear in for hundreds of yards. That's a tremendous distance when compared to the foods with the taste bruin most likes.

Sometimes trappers mix anise with molasses or the grain. Often, it is placed on a scent pad and used solely as a scent attractor with no provision for the bear to actually taste it. I don't figure it makes any difference if it is mixed in a food as long as it's there to help draw the bear in to the bait.

Anise, such as McCormick's brand, nestles in the spice rack of every grocery store. In a more concentrated form, drug stores carry it as a candy-making ingredient. Trapper supply houses, selling scent-making components and ingredients, sell anise in one-ounce bottles. The anise sold by the trapper supply houses has more strength of odor than that of the grocery store variety. Any anise smells of licorice and pulls in the bear. If using a weaker form of the scent, simply douse the bait or scent pad with more of it.

We've now gone over the best baits to pull in the old bruins, and one, fish, that despite its popularity, has some serious drawbacks. Now if you do use pork scraps instead of beef, the bear will forgive and work the bait. If fresh fish is kept at the bait, sure, the bear will dine with gusto. All baits, whether the recommended or the just-gettin'-by, have rules which need to be followed.

Meat baits with enough stench to wretch a maggot will draw a bear in to the bait. It attracts him. It is not good food for him. Once a bear hits a bait, once the bait is active, try to use fresh meat. Bad meat

Whether the grocery store or trapper supply variety, anise is an easy to obtain and use scent attractant for all black bear.

can make a bear sick. And a bear that has gotten sick over your bait will not come back. Bad bait can make a bear that sick — sick enough to drive him off the bait.

You can use tainted meat, meat with a stronger odor, to start your bait, but as soon as it's hit, try to keep the goods fresh. Pastries and grain, of course, will not go bad like meat baits.

Regardless of the type of bait, meat or sweet, you don't want to over feed the bear. An

Anise is a long distance call lure for bear. It can either be mixed with the bait or doused on a suspended scent pad.

overfed bear will get sick, too. It's like you loving chocolate fudge. One day, in some sort of pig-out mode, you eat and eat and eat chocolate fudge. You get sick that night. You get so sick that you cannot look another piece of chocolate fudge in the face for six years. If a bear eats so much off your bait that he gets sick and regurgitates, he won't be back. If a five-gallon bucket of bait does well, many folks figure two five-gallon buckets will double the bait site's effectiveness and draw.

No!

If the bear has enough to pig-out and get sick, you can actually kill that bait for that particular bear. No more than one five-gallon bucket of feed is needed per visit.

THE BAITING PROCESS

I saw my first bear bait in May of 1972, the year I graduated. For my graduation present, my dad took me with his brother, cousin, cousin's dad and friend above Cochrane, Ontario, to bear hunt— and to land several dozen good-sized northern pike.

The name and address of the person placing bear baits must be posted above each bait on a 2" x 4" tag.

The trip, a shoestring venture where we simply rented a cabin and a bait for each of us, was a real adventure. Everyone except me saw bear. Only cousin Bob got a shot. He drilled a bear between the eyes as it stared at him through a triangle of crossed sapling trunks.

To get to my bait, I balanced to the end of a boardwalk — single boards supported on the ends by log sections and traversing a swampy area. A 200 yard trail extended past the boardwalk's end. The trail snaked through thick cedar growth. The ground was like ski moguls with rounded mound next to rounded mound. On and between the mounds were cedars and tangles. Each cedar's trunk sprouted branches only inches above the ground. It was as thick a jungle of greenery as any rain forest. We could only imagine the complications and danger of following a wounded bear through such an impenetrable mass.

Finally, the trail entered a slightly open area. The cedar thinned at an intersection with another trail. This opening was about 30 yards in circumference and on one corner of the trail intersection. Two-thirds of the way across the opening from the trails' crossing stood a tall, thin tree. It was maybe eight inches in trunk diameter. About six feet above the ground the outfitter had lashed a cardboard box full of scraps. This was his baiting technique.

The outfitter, and I use this term loosely, simply tied boxes of scraps to various trees in the vicinity of his cabins. We were hunting the week after ice-out and the outfitter had just driven in the previous week from his job of prison guard in a California institution. He was working alone and obviously had not had an opportunity to have good baits out, let alone hot ones.

With the exception of cousin Bob's bear which was coming to a dump where Bob's bait was strung up, the other bear seen had nothing to do with the baits. For example, one in our party saw a bear on the other side of a beaver bog from him and the bait he was watching. The bear was grazing on grass. It was too far for a shot and the bait wasn't hit the entire week.

That was my first experience with bear baiting. Now, after much more experience, I don't feel the baits we hunted over that spring were more than a mediocre attempt to obtain U.S.A. dollars.

I've seen some Maine trappers in action. I've seen Maine outfitters and guides in action. I've interviewed a number of Maine trappers in whom I have a great deal of confidence. None of these folks tie up boxes. None of them would put paying hunters, or trappers, out on a week-old bait or a bait that wasn't being worked by at least one bear. Joe Baldwin pretty well sums up his baiting technique with this discussion:

"Legally here in the state of Maine you can't bait more than 30 days prior to the open season, so we start right around that 30 days. We used to bait all summer long, trying to find big bear. Now with that 30 day period, it's a little hit-and-miss and we'll run maybe three times as many baits the first two weeks just to find where the big bear are.

"And I like to be at least a month ahead of time. That way you'll get a bear working. My normal routine is to start out with 20 to 30 baits out the first two days we can legally bait. Let them set a week. Then I go back and take my tally of who hit what and where. When I find a big bear track or big bear scat, or that I'm relatively sure it's a big bear, then I'll start fine-tuning that down from going to the bait once a week to every four days, to three days, to two days, to every day — over a period of three weeks. Then just prior to setting a trap, we go about every day for a week — so that it's just like clockwork. The bears will get very regular. You get one coming at 4 o'clock in the afternoon, that's when he'll be there the next day — in most cases.

"Once I've found a good trophy bear on a bait, I really concentrate in that area with possibly one or two more baits in a two or three mile square radius.

"I like to start out with something that's a little smelly. Beaver carcasses that have some age on them, not necessarily figuring the bear's going to eat it, but at least I can get him into the area. I prefer to use beaver and beef as my meat-based scraps. And then I'll even use some cattle grain with a lot of molasses and sugar, water and anise mixed up with it. And then, as I'm fine-tuning those baits to either a hunter going on the bait or a trapper going on the bait, I'll come to the sweet foods, the pastry, the honey, use a lot of anise to get the smell out. But basically the bear has a sweet tooth. When we really want a bear to hold to an area, we'll use the sweets."

Except when you have a really big bear hitting a bait, don't set baits too close to each other. If a real bruiser is working a bait, as Joe stated, set out another one or two baits in a two or three square mile radius. That way, if for whatever reason, the trophy is spooked off of or simply quits the first bait, he'll probably already be working the others. That bear is not lost, but by a shift in strategy, can still be quickly bagged. Those extra baits ensure you stay in touch with him.

Some high-production (high-production of paying customers, that is) outfits set out baits every quarter of a mile. They'll then place hunters on each bait. The baits may all be hot baits getting hit daily, but, often by the same bear. Yes, the hunters all have a chance to take a bear, but if the bear is bagged, the other hunters remain sitting for the rest of the week on baits with little chance for contact with a bear.

For best results, scatter baits a minimum of two miles apart. Concentrate on finding different bear, not just on having as many baits as possible hit even if by the same bruin.

At the bait location, Joe digs a hole, I'd say about five-gallon bucket size. The scraps from his carrying bucket go in there. It, in effect, becomes the soup bowl where all the mixed grain and meat scraps wait for the bear to dine. Above or next to the bait hole, about five or six feet above the ground, a scent pad is tied. A sanitary napkin is the frequent lure holder. A swatch of cotton padding can also be used. The holder, whatever its form, is saturated with anise.

This is how the baits are initiated. Once the bait is hit and the bear needs to be drawn regularly to it, pastries are dumped in the bait hole, and a few tied up in two or three locations around the bait. Joe ties them up in sandwich bags. Small game of some sort almost always works the baits. Tying up a few pastries ensures that the bear will always have this most important of attractors awaiting him. It is effective. Joe has often had hunters over a bait confirm that before a bear visits the bait hole for his meal he beelines from sandwich bag to sandwich bag to have his dessert first.

Before leaving this section on baiting, let me reemphasize the important points:

1. Set baits, whenever possible, where major natural food sources and water are near each other — bait in the bear's living room, not just anywhere.

2. If baiting for a hunter, locate the bait with consideration for wind direction, noiseless access and open shooting lanes. For trapping purposes, baiting over solid bedrock or a boulder field is the only taboo. Wind direction, quiet access and openness of the area don't mean a thing.

3. The best meat-scrap baits are beaver and beef.

Dig a large hole to dump the bear bait in. Figure on using a five-gallon bucket of scraps and/or grain per visit.

4. The bear has a real sweet tooth. For bait start-up and maintenance, livestock grain with molasses greatly compliments the meat scraps.

5. Anise, whether mixed with the grain or, more commonly, doused on a scent holder, draws bear from a distance. Pork fat, too, is a good draw.

6. Use about one 5-gallon bucket of bait per visit. Too much can sicken a bear and he'll quit the bait never to return. Also, don't use rotten meat. Tainted meat will draw a bear from a further distance

than fresh grub, but as soon as a bear hits the bait, use fresh scraps.

7. Once a bear hits the bait, use pastries, cashing in on his sweet tooth, to hold him to regular visits.

8. Bait as early as possible with as many different baits scattered over as wide an area as possible. This is the only way to ensure good trails by big trophy bear when it's time to trap (or hunt).

Further information specific to Maine:

1. You cannot set baits within 500 yards of a dump.

2. Baits must have the name and address of the person placing them posted above them on a 2" x 4" tag.

3. Baits must be cleaned up when you are done with them so as not to violate littering laws.

4. Baits must be at least 50 yards from any travelway used by two-wheel or four-wheel vehicles.

The first step in successful bear trapping, or hunting, is proper baiting. *(Maine Dept. of Inland Fisheries and Wildlife)*

SETTING

The crisp edge of anticipation has stabbed the routine of placing and maintaining baits in the backwoods. Some baits have long since been abandoned for their lack of activity. Others have had an attraction for black bear ranging from occasional hits to nightly fiestas reminiscent of Mardi Gras in New Orleans. The observant and lucky bait tender will sometimes catch a glimpse of his quarry.

The bear can become very habituated to the daily visitor — especially if the time is consistent from day-to-day. Bring in the bait as normal, the same man with no visitor or friend to accompany him and foul the routine. Replenish the bait hole, refresh the anise pad, and hang those tasty sweets. Now, instead of melting back toward the vehicle, wait silently and hidden against some shadowed tree trunk. At some baits, a short 15 minute wait will be forgotten as a black shadow ambles down the trail toward the bait. The bear, having heard the daily bait run, waited a polite quarter hour, then moved in for the vittles.

Fresh sign of a large bear on a bait that is getting hit every day answers the dreams of the trapper. After enough activity to grow bear trails radiating from the bait, it's only a matter of waiting for the season opener. Actually seeing the bruin gives more incentive to an already full charge of adrenaline and anticipation.

The baits working and the calendar finally reading the opening date, the trapper digs in his sets. All the important baiting work done so far has simply gotten the trapper in touch with the bear. That contact is paramount. Without it, failure is all too frequent. With it, success is close to attained. For all this, on the act of setting the trap and its placement hangs the balance of success.

Setting the Foot-snare: Step-by-step

TOP VIEW   SIDE VIEW

 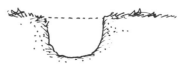

1. Dig a hole slightly smaller in diameter than the snare loop and 12 to 18 inches deep, the deeper the better.

2. Dig a slot to the side for the spring mechanism. It need only be half to a third as deep as the main hole.

 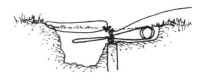

3. Place the spring mechanism, set it, engage the spring safety and lay the loop. The spring needs to be set at least three inches below the surrounding ground level, four to five inches is better.

 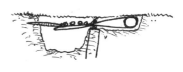

4. Stick pencil-sized sticks into the hole sides with so the free ends are laying on the trigger. These are on the same level as the trigger. (Note: No loop is shown on the side view for purposes of illustration.)

5. Place a round clump of spaghum moss over the trigger so it just fills the hole in circumference. Release the spring safety, then camouflage the spring with leaves and bits of ground debris.

SETTING THE FOOT-SNARE

T he entire structure and purpose of the foot-snare aims at throwing a cable loop up and around a bear's foot as the loop closes in size. The following steps will ensure the greatest odds of that happening with efficiency:

1. PREPARE THE TRAP BED. "Trap bed" is a trapping term describing the evacuation or resting place of a trap set for a quarry. For land-based animals such as bobcat or fox, the trap must be "bedded" in a trap bed so it is solid, won't tip and won't rock. If it does, the target animal may either back off from this unnatural underfoot sensation or else dig up the trap to see what's making that funny wiggly motion under its paw. And contrary to first thought, a critter that's digging up a set trap rarely gets caught.

The physical trap bed and the act of bedding the trap combine as a great dividing factor between mediocre trappers and great trappers. If a trapper, so-so in other respects, can punch in rock solid sets, he will probably out-produce the otherwise above average outdoorsman

The first step in setting a foot-snare is to enlarge the cable loop as large as it will go. Lay it on the ground where you want to set it (right). With the loop as a guide, mark a circle slightly inside the cable with the trowel (below). This tracing is the size of hole to dig.

who can only plant wobbly, tippy sets.

The first step in setting a foot-snare is to dig a hole. When the bear steps into the center of the hole, it trips the trigger and finds the loop thrown up around its leg. To expedite this sequence, the hole needs to be slightly less in diameter than the diameter of the fully enlarged foot-snare loop. When set the loop will lay on the ground, so that slightly smaller hole size is necessary. Too large a hole and the loop has nothing to lay on. Too small a hole and the bear will not be able to step into it properly. Measure the hole by placing the opened snare loop on the appropriate spot on the ground and cutting an outline inside the loop with the trapper's trowel. Keep the trowel about an inch from the loop. Now remove the loop and begin making that hole inside the outline.

The hole needs to be deep. The deeper the better. Make it at least 12" deep. The foot-snare trigger will be at least 3" under the level of the surrounding ground. Four to five inches below the ground level is better. This allows room for a moss covering and for the bear to be stepping as far as possible below the ground level — this helps get a high grip when the spring throws up the cable loop. With the trigger setting so deep, there must be additional depth below it. When the bear's weight pushes down the trigger, you want air under it — not a shallow hole that will stop its downward swing before the spring is released.

This hole needs to have straight sides. Don't form it into a reverse cone. Keep it wide and open all the way to the bottom. Here is where hitting one of those rocks that Maine is so famous for can thwart the resolve of the toughest mountain man. A fiery sun setting on the distant mountain while you're punching hole after hole trying to find a soft enough spot to sink one foot-snare can make you want to cry. Yep, rocks are tough.

If there are no rocks too large to dig around and remove, then tree roots frequently hinder the evacuation. A pair of hand pruners make easy work of smaller roots. A few snips and you've got a clean hole.

This main hole needs some additional excavating. A trench needs dug to accomodate the snare's spring. Dig the trench at right angles to the bear's expected line of travel. This is easy to figure at a trail set or at a walk-through cubby. Lay the spring down so the anchoring prongs are even with the edge of the main hole. Now go a little past the coil hinge of the spring for the end measurement. Dig this out so

Dig the main hole deep (right) Keep the sides straight all the way to the bottom. After the main hole is dug, dig a trench from the side to hold the spring.

it's as deep as you want the trigger in the main hole, probably four to five inches deep. The width need not be great, maybe three inches.

The finished foot-snare bed has the shape of a long-handled pot sunk into the ground. Throw the rocks and soil taken from the hole and trench away from the set.

2. ANCHOR THE TRAP. Wisdom of experience teaches you to anchor the trap before bedding it. An anchored trap won't mess up the setting process, but anchoring — particularly if it's a stretch to reach the anchor — can disturb or set off the finished set.

A tree, not too hard a commodity to locate in bear country, makes the best anchor. It should be 8" or more in diameter. Most bear trails will brush at least one solid, thick tree to wrap the cable around.

Always use a hard wood tree, not necessarily a hardwood. Quaking aspen, for example, classified as a hardwood, have about as much staying power when up against bear teeth as a scoop of ice cream in the August sun. A solid oak tree or beech, in good health, and not rotten or dead, will withstand the brunt of the bear's attacks.

Too thin a tree, or a soft or rotten one, and the bear will gnaw it until his escape is made. And make sure it is at least 8" in diameter. Softer woods should even be larger to ensure that trophy-of-a-lifetime remains tethered.

The ideal tree won't sprout branches for at least the first six or so feet up. This is far less important than the heft and hardiness of the trunk.

If it reaches, circle the manufacturer's installed anchoring cable around the tree trunk. If it won't reach, then clamp on an extension cable of the appropriate length. Wrap the cable around the trunk only one time. The loop should be loose enough after clamping so it will revolve around the tree as the cable (the bear in the snare) is pulled around the tree. This slight looseness and movement acts as a swiveling point. The bear will be able to walk to Mars and back around that tree without winding the cable down to a no-movement tautness.

Don't make that cable too loose around the tree. Make it just free enough to pull around the trunk. If the cable is too loose, the bear might climb the tree and pull the entire affair after him. A bear wrapped up more than ten feet from the ground is a predicament to say the least. He's tougher to get a clean shot into, and he can be a bugger to get down. A climbing bear who gets tangled up at some height can do a lot of self-inflicted damage. Test the anchoring loop after tightening the clamps and make sure it can't be slipped or walked up the trunk.

If at all possible, anchor to a single tree. Craig McLaughlin, a biologist doing a lot of bear work for the Maine Fish and Game Department, will even cut down a tree or two to isolate the one to which he anchors. If you can keep the bear from climbing and from reaching other trees with his solid grasp, he'll not have anything to fight. Such a bear can't do anything. He'll simply walk in circles forever.

Bear trappers often anchor with drags because they can be placed anywhere you want to plant a set. Live trees, of course, are where you find them.

Before placing and setting the trap, anchor it. The best anchor is a solid tree of hard wood (top, opposite page). After anchoring, check the cable (bottom, opposite page). The cable around the trunk should be snug enough to prevent a bear from pulling it upward, yet just loose enough to allow the cable to swivel around the tree.

Cut bear drags from green, hard wood trees or from dead timber whose integrity has not been compromised by decay. I've seen drags of lesser dimensions, but I'd recommend a drag of ten feet in length and no less than eight inches in diameter. Remember, bear will "eat" rotten or soft wood. Use only solid drags.

Take two wraps of the anchoring cable around the middle of the drag. Keeping these wraps as tight as possible, rachet down the clamps. You want no free play on the two wraps around the drag.

Like a raccoon, a bear on a drag will generally fight harder than one on a solid anchor. And just as with a tree anchored foot-snare with too loose a wrap around the tree trunk, a bear hooked to a drag might climb a nearby tree. That's always a nuisance which can escalate into a real big problem. For these reasons, use a tree anchor if possible.

But, there's an even more important reason for a rooted tree preference. One Maine trapper, who will remain nameless for our purposes, had a bear trap tied to a drag. The set guarded a bait at the end of a 200-yard long trail. The trap, unlike the better trail set, was at the bait itself.

Well, the bait, fed on regularly by a nice black bear, paid off. One night, the trapper in question knows not the exact hour, the bear stepped on the soft moss over the trigger. The spring flew debris and the snare loop upward. The startled black bear jumped back, but not with the speed of spring steel. The cable loop encircled his foreleg. The jerking action of the bear drew the loop tight as it slipped back down toward his claws and the bear was tethered — almost like a hobbled mountain horse near a Rocky Mountain outfitter's spur camp.

Before dawn, the bear had rolled with the drag and had boxed many rounds with the snags and brush. He finally rested in a bit of cover near the trapper's access path. He wasn't near the bait any more. The big bruin was taking his rest a mere 50 yards from the pulloff where the trapper parked his truck.

This trapper had the normal morning expectations. Still, he was only halfway through his first cup of coffee and only half awake. He parked his truck and did a weird concoction of half walk, half shuffle down the path. He was little more than sleep walking — and he hadn't even loaded his gun.

The bear, hearing the truck come to a halt a measley 50 yards along the path, simply hunkered down more in his resting place. He

The best drags are green. Fresh-cut drags are solid and less likely to be chewed due to decay or brittleness. Bow saws are the most efficient, quiet and safe way to cut bear drags (above). Unlike anchoring snares to standing trees, use a double wrap around a drag and cinch it as tight as possible (right). You don't want the cable slipping off the drag!

was surely working his adrenaline back up to maximum level as his ears heard the lone woodsman approaching. A bear, even a normally docile black bear, quickly builds up a horrendous mountain of raging, bristling hate when put into a compromising situation. Being held against his will in a foot-snare while his most feared opponent, man, approaches surely puts him into a fit.

As the trapper casually and unexpectedly worked his way down the narrow path through the brush, the bear's small, squinted black eyes burned at the approach of his enemy — all the surging adrenaline and hate and rage focusing on that lone, puny man.

The trapper skirted a small bush and stepped over a fallen birch trunk. In mid-step, he got a jolt with an edge sharper than the perk from a gallon of strong java. While his left foot was making its arch over the black-scarred bark, a little to his left and only 23 feet away, an innocent and surprisingly small bush exploded in a fury.

The black bear, the frustration of his entire night's restraint combined with the renewed power spawned of being cornered by an approaching enemy, put every fiber of muscle, slobbering jaws and bristling hair into a hard drive to the trapper. The trapper hadn't a chance. Even if his gun had been loaded, the shortness and suddenness of the attack would have left no time for an unprepared man to react. If the trapper had moved in alert, gun ready, he'd have had time for a quick, but telling shot. But a half awake man with an unloaded gun? Such a man outrunning or outclimbing a maniacal bear? No way. Before his foot hit the ground, the trapper knew he was in for it. It's amazing the way the human computer can put so much through the mind in even a split second. In less time than it takes to read even one of these sentences, the carefree trapper was transformed into an energetic, bounding prey species who reacted as quickly as any whitetail deer. Of course, the bound wasn't as high or wide as a deer's, but the effort was still spectacular.

Before his foot had cleared that birch log, the trapper saw the bear launch from the bush. It appeared as black death with all the power and drive and size of a locomotive. It came eyes beady and red, growling loud enough to burst ear drums, and teeth popping in the characteristic of every charging bear.

Before the trapper had landed from that first frantic, heart-pounding-through-the-throat-and-against-the-top-of-the-skull bound, the bear piled up into a mass of flailing legs, black fur and flying debris. The cable, with the prayers of a lifetime being answered, held. It was wrapped around several snags and tree trunks making a solid anchor. The bear reached the end of his tether and was rolled when snubbed. The old boar ravaged his surroundings and glared at the retreating trapper between continued efforts to throw himself toward his rival. If there had been a way, the trapper would not have lived to see the second half of his coffee.

Amid shakes making loading and aiming almost impossible, the

Though often appearing passive when first approached, a trapped black bear is a powerful and unpredictable opponent. Don't let appearances deceive you into a false sense of security. A bear can change his demeanor instantly and viciously. Most can be handled with no problem, but you never know which one will react dangerously ... or when! *(Maine Dept. of Inland Fisheries & Wildlife)*

trapper gingerly worked to a large tree about 25 feet from the bear. He shot, and his luck holding, it went true and the bear died quickly. The bear lay six feet outside the bush from which he had launched his attack — a good 17 feet from where trapper had stepped over the fallen birch. But if the round cable holding the three toes hadn't held? Or if the log drag had not been snubbed tight?

This nameless trapper was extremely lucky. The danger over, he had learned a valuable lesson about drags and trapped bear. Bears on drags can be anywhere! You check dragged sets with the utmost caution — always — even on the day you've given up and are going in to pull the set.

A Pennsylvania buddy of mine went to Maine to trap a bruin. He used drags only. His guide showed a good dose of deserved caution. The drags were placed so they could be seen from quite a distance. You can't always see that a set has been sprung and the trap and drag gone until you're right up on it. By thinking ahead, you can place the drag so it is most easily seen from down the trapper's path. You can even lean it against a tree. If on your approach you see the drag is no longer leaning or lying where it should be, then instantly double your guard.

My friend? He got his bear, a nice one. On the third check day, they immediately saw that the drag was missing. Both got their guns ready. If a bear bent on tearing off your flesh materializes from a nearby clump of ferns, it's no time to quibble over whether the guide or the trapper should shoot.

They moved in slowly, still hunting in effect — moving a few steps, looking all around and then taking another few steps. They finally spied the bear a little ways off. They safely approached and finished the deed.

Take this as a firm warning about the possibility of a bear on a drag tying up or resting close to the trapper's access path. A bear doesn't do this with malicious intent. It is strictly coincidental. Beginning as a coincidence won't render hand-to-paw combat with a black bear any less harmful. Such an encounter adds immeasurably to your future tales — and to your hospital bills.

3. SETTING THE FOOT-SNARE. The foot-snare's triggering assembly has a set of wire prongs that get pushed into the ground to hold it. The top wire of the spring has a hook in it for the cable to lay in. The cable has a heavy cast swivel connecting the snare cable to the anchoring cable. Take the wire prong on the loop side of the spring hook and thread it through the swivel eye. Having the swivel anchored by the prong helps arm the trap. When the trap is sprung, the spring throws the snare loop upward. Since the swivel is solidly held by a prong, the loop is decreased in size as it rises. The loop, then, not only rises up the bear's limb, but is tightened as it does so. (See the picture on page 43 to see the positioning of the swivel in the prong.)

The prong in the swivel, push the prongs into the bottom of the trench where it meets the main hole. Done properly, the spring will lay in the trench and the trigger will extend into the center of the main hole.

Now fold the hook end of the spring toward the trigger. Depress the spring, lift the trigger, and latch it over the end of the spring hook. Put on the safety hook so it holds the spring together. This will keep the spring, if it should spring during the setting, from hitting you in the face or throwing dirt in your eyes. The trigger should be a good 4" down in the main hole and parallel to the ground level. The set spring

For the snare loop to close properly on the bear's paw, the swivel needs to be threaded on the seating prong. Use the prong which is on the bend side of the spring hook.

With the swivel on the prong, push the device's seating prongs into the ground where the main hole and the trench join. The spring should lay in the trench.

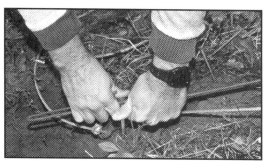

Here's what the foot-snare looks like when the prongs are push-ed into the ground. The spring and trigger are not yet set and the loop not yet in place.

Bend the spring over and pull up the trigger so the trigger latch pivots over the spring's end-hook (above). Still holding the trigger upward, hook the spring safety (left). Pull the loop cable into the spring end-hook with the snare lock on the loop side of the end-hook (below).

Enlarge the cable loop to its maximum size (above) and lay it around the hole. The set foot-snare ready for camouflaging (below).

should be laying at the bottom of the trench.

Place the loop cable into the spring hook. If the swivel is skewered by the correct prong, the cable will come up from the swivel and lay over the spring wire at the hook. If the wrong prong holds the swivel, you'll be trying to push the cable into the hook without it having to cross the spring wire — and it'll fall out of the hook on the slightest whim. Be sure the proper prong holds the swivel so the cable will cross the upper spring wire as it lays in the spring hook and be securely held.

With the cable in the spring hook, open the cable loop as large as possible. This slides the cable lock along the cable until it is snug up against the spring hook. This sliding cable lock, then, stays on the loop side of the spring hook while resting against the spring hook. Lay the rest of the cable loop on the ground so it encircles the main hole.

4. COVERING THE TRAP. The foot-snare is now set. Everything is in place to do its job. Now everything needs covered, camouflaged, so the bear will step on the trigger and be in the ideal position for the foot-snare to get a good hold.

Take pencil-sized sticks, broken from dead branches or cut with snips of the hand pruners, and stick them into the side of the main hole. One end of each stick is pushed into the side of the main hole. The other end rests on the trigger itself. It is critical that the sticks be level with the plane of the trigger. For this reason, stick the ends into the hole side at the same height as the trigger. Obviously, take care in placing the sticks so the trigger isn't sprung.

Take sticks the size of pencils and poke them into the side of the hole (above). Rest the free ends on the trigger. Five sticks and this foot-snare is ready for the camouflaging cover (below—seen from spring end).

Position about five or six sticks. The exact number isn't too important. The end result is to have them look like spokes of a wheel when looking down into the hole. The spoked-wheel combination of trigger and sticks will support the next very critical phase of setting the foot-snare.

Even though a black bear has a big, heavy, padded foot, he doesn't like to step on anything that's sharp, humpy, a rock, or anything like that. You can make them step where you want because they don't like to step on such objects.

Spaghnum moss, prolific in boggy spots, is the best covering for the foot-snare's (or foot-gripper's) trigger. It actually invites the bear to place his foot on its cushy softness.

Trim the edge of the sphagnum moss clump until it is the right diameter (left). Place it carefully over the trigger (and stick supports) and tuck the moss inside the hole edges (above).

Applying this trait directly to trap covering, a soft covering over the trap trigger gives the bear the soft, quiet stepping spot he favors. Give him a guaranteed soft spot to step on and he will step there. You will be directing his foot to the exact spot it needs to step in order to get a good catch.

The number one covering to fulfill this important mission is spaghnum moss. I don't have a close second. Even if the moss isn't natural to the area being trapped, the bear will sink his big paw into that round patch of lush green. Since spaghnum moss won't be growing everywhere you want to place a bear set, keep an eye peeled for it around wet boggy areas. Spaghnum moss is lusher and softer than most other mosses. It grows in colonies of closely growing, fluffy plumes. The hidden base of the plumes is very pale, sometimes a dirty white. The easily visible portion of the plume is a pale green. Other mosses I'm familiar with all have a dark or bright green color.

When this special moss is found, push your fingers down into one side of a clump, work your fingers around in a circle as you push down into the base of the moss. This circle should be a good 14" or so across. Continue to work around and then under the moss clump until it is finally freed from the ground it's growing on.

Now's the time to camouflage the snare loop with leaves, pine needles and other woods debris. Put this on sparsely. The purpose is to blend in the cable, not bury it.

Dig up and carry a number of these, including spares. You can carry them in the back of a pickup or in a box. If not used that day, it would be wise to keep them damp and covered.

Carry a clump to the set site before making the set. When the "wheelspoke" sticks are in place on the trigger, lift up the spaghnum clump. Carefully work around it. Pull off any odd protrusions of moss. You don't want peninsulas of moss hanging over the cable loop. Also, tear off the perimeter of the moss portion-by-portion until the remaining nucleus can just be tucked into the main hole of the set. You don't want a wad of dirt underneath the moss, but don't take off so much that the moss clump falls into a bag full of pieces. Do all the trimming carefully so the clump to be used will keep together in a solid mass and not disintegrate.

The doctoring of the moss done, gingerly position it on the trigger and the "spoke" sticks. Tuck the edges down so they are all well within the hole sides. That is the trigger covering. The covering, as critical as it is, is that simple. The moss disc, like a luminous, light-green full moon mesmerizing pixies, will pull down the bear's pad to its softness.

If moss is unavailable, use sod with the dirt knocked off—a soft footing. Stay away from crunchy leaves and other noisy coverings.

After the moss carpets the hole immediately over the trigger, you can take leaves and other fine forest debris to finish blending in the set. Sprinkle a little on the cable loop and the spring. Trapping bear is like trapping giant raccoon, not fox. You do not need to wear gloves or dye your traps to hid foreign odors. You also do not need to be super clever in concealing every part of the trap and cable. Just blend it in a little.

IMPORTANT: *Before camouflaging the spring and trench, carefully flip off the spring safety hook.* Forget this and you'll cry when the big boy you're after perfectly targets the moss covering, while the spring continues its vigil as useless as teats on a boar hog. Take that safety off!

I use moss fragments to loosely fill in the trench around the spring. I sprinkle leaf debris over this. It's a temptation to use spaghnum moss to camouflage the entire cable loop, trap and spring. It does such an excellent job — but don't do it. To do so would be an invitation for the bear to step elsewhere at the set. Keep the nice moss stepping pad unique to the circle down in the hole and over the trigger. Don't bother to camouflage the anchoring cable or any extensions.

5. THE FINISHED SET. The set is, in essence, finished. It will take bear. You can move on with confidence that the job was well done. You might even sleep poorly that night because you just "know" you'll have that hit in the morning and will walk in to a trophy. But if you are like the best fur and nuisance control trappers, you'll not yet be satisfied with the set. You'll need to fine-tune it for every practical possibility.

Experienced trappers know that a hundred-and-one unexpected longshots and quirks can destroy all their dreams of a catch. Moisture from the ground can penetrate the dirt covering of a land set, freeze and leave the set like concrete — the targetted coyote dancing all over the set and not springing it. A mink, with his very short legs, because of a mere 2" rise in water swims over the carefully planned set instead of stepping on the trap pan. A fisher, travelling his ten-day circuit, with no apparent reason, picks this time to cross through a pine point

Jamming a stick into the ground next to the juncture of spring and trigger will ensure that the bear won't step on that critical spot. If a bear steps there, he'll trip the trap without his foot being in the proper place for a sure catch. In this photo, stepping sticks are already in place in front of and behind the snare.

a hundred feet upwind of his last trip's path. In doing so, he avoids the trapper's set which had been so pain-stakingly placed. And only a trapper can suffer the let down of seeing a beaver track on silt which had settled in a fine film over the trap pan — the trap pan being held permanently up so it can't be tripped because a chip of wood from the beaver's tree felling had fatefully floated and wedged under the pan. I could go one indefinitely. I've lived these and have heard of totally unbelievable twists which hinder the trapper's best efforts. For all of this, for all of the unexpected, you don't leave a set in okay condition. You fine-tune it against every practical contigency. So, too, must the bear trapper.

The first bit of fine-tuning is to ensure that part of the bear's paw won't be partially over the spring end, the hook. If it is, the bear's weight might keep the spring down until the bear is already lifting that paw — foiling the loop throw. And obviously, if any of his paw, even a toe or claw, is over the spring hook, then the cable cannot possibly lift up and around the entire paw.

To remedy this, take advantage of the bear's abhorance of stepping on sharp objects. Snap off a few sharp sticks and stick them into the ground so the points aim upward. They should be next to the spring and just outside the loop. A bear won't step there now.

If the trap site isn't naturally narrowed down, then you probably

Place a stepping stick on the trail on either side of the foot-snare. Place them right up next to the cable's edge.

Each stepping stick should be two to three inches in diameter and five or six feet long. Make sure they won't be easy for the bear to brush aside. IMPORTANT: Suspend the sticks two to three inches above the ground so the bear won't step ON them, but will step between them.

Here's a completed foot-snare set (top view). Note the stepping stick positioning in relationship to the moss trigger covering. Both sides of the trail have a little brush poked into the ground to further funnel the bear's foot over the trigger.

should make sure it is. A natural narrowing is best, so the bear has no other way to follow the trail but to step on the set. Sparser than normal undergrowth or the narrow spots being impossible to set because a hole can't be dug there, demands setting in trails that have a lot of area to the right and to the left. Narrow such spots down.

Take brushy limbs, especially crackly, dry limbs, and stick them into the ground or pile them up so they fence the sides off. Don't over do this. The bear, by his habitual nature, will want to follow the trail he, himself, has made. The barricading of the sides by the trapper is not to bulldog a hard-headed bruin into submission, but rather is to give him a further nudging to continue to do as he has been. You're just telling him he was right from the beginning.

I always place a little brush on the spring assembly. Don't hinder the spring, but ensure that it won't be stepped on anywhere along its length.

When the cable has been camouflaged, I like to reinforce the placement of the paw over the trap. We've already narrowed the left to right possibilities. Now, the forward and backward placement should be controlled. Whether a natural stepping stick exists or not, such as a tree root the bear is already stepping over, place one of your own both in front of and behind the set.

Place the sticks so they are almost over the respective side of the cable loop. Don't cover the loop, but just come to it with the side of the stepping stick. The stepping sticks should be about two or three inches in diameter and suspended slightly above the ground. The bear might feel a larger stick will hold his weight and step on the stick, never placing a paw on the moss covering. By suspending the stick slightly, propping an end on some brush or a nearby log, the bear won't step on it. A bear doesn't like to step on sticks or small diameter logs that don't rest on the ground — they might give way under his weight. Place these stepping sticks so they are about two to three inches above the ground. That's all it takes.

Use stepping sticks of fair length, maybe five or six feet long. Don't make them easy for the bear to brush aside if he, for whatever reason, would decide to do so.

THE TRAIL SET

The setting techniques just covered, though applicable to all foot-snaring, were specifically tailored to the trail sets. Most bear trapping, especially effective bear trapping will be trail setting. Most often the trails where the foot-snare is concealed will be bear trails radiating from bear baits. Sometimes trails leading to natural food crops, such as corn or orchards, will be set up.

The most obvious question here is what does a bear trail look like? How can you tell if a path through the woods is, indeed, a bear trail?

First of all, when I say bear trail, I'm speaking of trails made by the bear and regularly used by the bear. A tote road through the brush that a bear might travel once or twice a week, is not a bona fide bear trail. Honest to goodness bear trails will be found around concentrated food sources. These trapper baits, cornfields, berry patches and so on are the only locations a bear will travel on such a regular basis to pad down a distinct trail.

Let's say you do find a distinct trail where you would expect it to have been pounded down by the regular travels of a bear. How do you ascertain that its existence is because of a bear? It could, in reality, be a porcupine or raccoon trail. A foot-snare built on such a small game trail may look mighty fine, but it won't snag you many bruins.

A bear track finishes the question. Unfortunately, though, the trails I've seen have rarely had surfaces which would take a bear print. If the trail seems to be a bear trail, follow it a ways. If it is truly a bear trail, there should be bear scat somewhere along it. Find bear droppings along the trail and you're relatively sure a bear will be back along that trail.

The scats, during the fall when the bear eats a lot of apples and such, may have a lot of diahrrea. It's easily distinguished from deer and moose pellets, and from small game droppings. For further

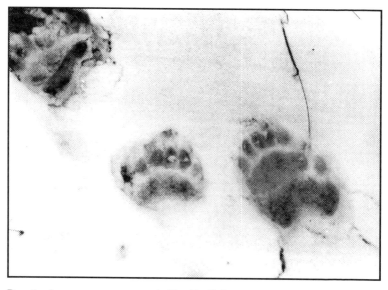

Bear tracks on snow are a snap to identify. Unfortunately, few bear tracks can be identified on the typical Maine bear trapline. You have to read other sign to identify a bear trail.

information on bear scats, tracks and sign, get a copy of the #9 volume of the Peterson Field Guide series. Number 9 is *ANIMAL TRACKS* by Olaus J. Murie.

If you're not really sure that the trail is a bear trail and sign cannot be found, then force some sign. Normally, a bear will reach up and mark trees. A lot of bear coming to a bait will mark trees. They reach up as far as they can with their claw and scrape down a tree, or even bite into the bark with their teeth. If you just can't find sign to ascertain the trail being investigated is a bear trail, mix some sugar water with anise. Splash this on a tree somewhere along that trail. The bear will really mark up that tree with their clawing. You can add a little beaver castor to the mixture, too.

Don't figure that trails radiating from a bait or food source will be traveled 100% by bear or 100% by

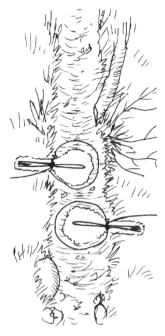

In nuisance control or biological studies where trap limits are not a concern, double setting on trails can tilt the odds even more in the trapper's favor.

small game. Such absolutes rarely happen. Don't take one bear scat on some two-track woods road or a coyote track along a trail as gospel. Sure the scat or track might indicate a trail used primarily by that particular species. But it might also be sign of a single erratic passing, with some other critter being the main user.

If bear are definitely hitting the bait — it's easy to tell because of bear scat, the bait and bait hole being ravaged by large claws, and hung pastries being torn down — then it's safe and standard practice to assume that newly formed trails at that bait are bear trails. The additional sign of tracks, scat and tree marking confirm.

Figuring trails has little scientific background. It's simply looking at the trail's location (relationship to a nearby food source), observing sign present, maybe acting as a catalyst to have fresh sign created, and going with gut feeling. It's all part of the adventure.

The narrowest spot a trail goes through is the best place to set.

Where the path snakes through thick brush gives the bear no option but to travel directly over the trap. Aside from concealing the trap, the trapper only has to set up stepping sticks in order to funnel the paw directly on the trigger.

Trail restrictions, of course, work only if the ground can be dug for trap bedding. Also, unless a drag is to be used, a suitable tree to anchor to must be close

I wouldn't set right on a bait. I'd go down the trail 20 feet or more. Just as trails funnel incoming bear to the bait, when right up at the bait the bear may diverge — going to different hung pastries or some other attraction. Make sure the set is concealed on the main trail beyond the point where any bear's approach to the bait may be fanning out.

THE DIRTHOLE SET

The dirthole set automatically conjures up visions of long-line canine trappers, particularly fox trappers. When the dirthole set was first made public to trappers in general, it was heralded as the most important discovery and secret of the fox trapper. The fox or coyote trapper makes a dirthole by digging a 45 degree hole at the base of a small mound or tuft of grass. This hole may be around two to three inches in diameter and anywhere from five to seven inches deep. Bait is concealed at the back of this hole. The trapper dribbles some lure in the hole or on the backing it was dug against. Often fox or coyote urine is sprinkled around the set. A concealed trap closely guards the front of the hole. With its multitude of variations, this was and still is one of the most effective sets for canines. It is also very effective for bobcat, raccoon, skunk, opossum, wolf and many other critters, including bear.

Dirtholes effectively take black bear. Foot-snares and bear targets require quite a variation from the standard fox- and coyote-sized sets.

Art Bousquet frequently uses them for both sport trapping and nuisance control: *"My basic one is the dirthole set. It's made just like you would for fox, except you put a one-pound coffee can in the hole. You put the snare right over the hole. The bear will reach in ...*

"A lot of guys tell you it's no good because the bear shove their nose down in, the spring hits them in the nose, and all it does is spook them. The secret to it is to dig a deep hole so he can't touch the trigger with his nose.

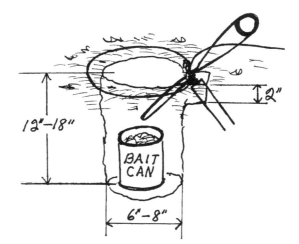

Art Bousquet's dirthole set for bear. Note the angle of the snare spring and trigger. These are critical to prevent misses.

"Dig down 18 inches to two feet, straight down — don't angle the hole.

"You can pour bacon right down the hole, but I prefer to have a one-pound coffee can in the bottom because I put molasses, honey or whatever I happen to be using right in it.

"I lay the cable right on the ground around the hole.

"Okay, now here's the secret. You put the trigger facing down in the hole. You angle it, I'd say at ... oh, I wouldn't go 45, but between 45 and 25 degrees. I have no set thing, I just tilt it down into the hole. The reason I do that is when he sticks his nose down in there to sniff it, if he hits the trigger, it'll go off in his face. If it's down in the hole, he'd have to shove his head way down the hole. You only make the hole a little bigger than a pound coffee can, so that he's got to put his foot down in.

"Another thing I do is I take sharpened little sticks and stick them into the side of the hole, facing up, especially where the trigger is. He'll stick his nose down in that stick, about the size of a pencil, and it'll poke him. Their nose is more touchy than their feet. When he reaches in there with his paw, he just pushes the sticks right out of the way. That's nothing to him — but he won't stick that in his mouth or nose.

"Where the spring prongs anchor the spring, I dig down an inch or two before sticking them in. The spring part sticks up in the air, facing the hole. That's what you've got to be careful about. Don't get *it in front of the hole. You're tilting that trigger down, making the spring come up higher, so you've got to put the spring to one side. You've got to make sure the spring isn't between the bear and the hole. I pile brush up or set the spring next to bushes, so the bear won't come toward the spring side of the hole. The bushes at the set, or the brush I place, makes the bear come in so the spring is to the side."*

Art has a lot of confidence in this set. His record of taking as many as 12 bear in one season (nuisance control for the Fish and Wildlife Department) speaks for itself. Keep the dirthole set in your battery of options.

Use the dirthole set in two situations: hit baits with no good trails, and trapping with no trails or baits.

What if the bait was regularly being hit by bear, but no good trail could be found? In other words, there just wasn't a trail set available. Here's where I'd not hesitate to plug in a dirthole set. I'd make it fairly close to the bait, too. Maybe four to six feet away. Being a baited set, you might have more trouble with small game tripping the snare. If so, just reset and wait for the bear.

Particularly if cold-rolling, whether beginning to set out your own baits or looking for natural locations, I'd immediately place dirthole sets anywhere I found fairly fresh bear sign. You probably won't have any trails to set up with this kind of trapping, but until you do, the dirthole sets might get you a quick bonus. I don't feel setting up good trails next to hot baits can be equalled. The bear are out there somewhere, though, and dirthole sets might get your bear tag filled even before the baits are hit.

THE CUBBY SET

A bear-sized cubby is a monstrous affair. It's like a cabin with two end walls missing. This allows the bear to see through and actually to walk through the cubby. It is often called a walk-through cubby to distinguish it from a cubby with only one opening.

Build the cubby with two walls of logs or large saplings. The walls should be about three feet apart, three or four feet high, and at least three feet long. Cover the top with other logs and debris. Place bait in the cubby. Place the trap so the bear will step on the trigger when walking through the cubby.

Cubbies are effective. They require a lot of work to build and don't increase your odds much over the other methods outlined in this book. One big advantage of them is their additional safety factor when using steel-jawed bear traps. Cubbies also have an aesthetic appeal with those wishing to identify with the past days of the mountain men and pioneers. This nostalgia must be weighed with the tremendous amount of work even a single cubby requires.

A transient trapper wouldn't be the one to build a cubby. These more or less permanent structures are more the property of a trapline to be used year after year. They, therefore, would be the domain of the resident trapper.

I bring up the cubby for the same reason as discussion of the steel-jawed trap. It will broaden the scope of the bear trapper's knowledge. It may be a technique which a few may wish to try. For the trapper wishing for effective, streamlined methods? Stick to trail sets as the primary set and dirtholes for situations where trail sets won't work.

SETTING THE NECK SNARE

I asked one experienced western trapper, a trapper who declines to become a celebrity thus remaining nameless, who had experience with both foot-snares and neck snares, which one was more effective. His immediate response was neck snares:

"It's much, much easier to get a bear to poke his head through a snare. His feet? He doesn't lift them very far off the ground. He shuffles. His head is fairly low. He's used to pushing forward with his chest. He's used to using his face to push through brush and stuff. He has small eyes and small ears, so he just rams through. So it seems to be very, very simple and doesn't take any special finagling, whereas with the foot-snare you've got to put out a bait, you've got to establish a pattern, you've got to get them to put their feet just so. You've got to position the trigger ... you know what I'm saying? It's more critical."

Remember, neck snares are legal only in some locations for nuisance control work where live capture and relocation is either impractical or undesirable. They are not legal in Maine for sport trapping. For the curious and for those in nuisance control, let's take a look at effective bear neck snaring. Our nameless trapper continues:

"The Thompson is a popular snare — the timber wolf size. The

bear are real easy to neck snare. In fact, the first one I ever got, I didn't even know I had him. He hit the snare and took off about 15 feet with the drag in the bushes, wrapped around a tree and died. Bang! Just like that.... and the ground wasn't even torn up. He raked the bushes a little bit, he had some scratches on the trees, but I was amazed at how simple it was.

"Bear travel with their head low and you look for a real narrow spot in the trail. There's all kinds of places where bear go under stuff. They're not afraid to duck under or to crawl through stuff.

""I try to find a natural duck stick. At one set I had—it was in raspberries, and it was pretty obvious—you could see where they were walking, shuffling through. So I just lifted the top of the snare into the raspberries and made it wide enough, about 13" to 14" in diameter, and they were all caught by the neck.

"The loop height is similar to snaring coyotes ... maybe seven to eight inches from the ground to the bottom of the snare loop.

"I got two bear on running poles. The poles were each an eight to ten inch diameter spruce I knocked down onto another one, wedging at about a 45 degree angle. I took the snare and supported it with a support wire (a thick, stiff wire, maybe 12 gauge, that is pinched on the snare wire next to the lock and is bent to hold the loop in the proper position — editor) where a couple of limbs stuck out on each side. I placed the snare so the bottom of the loop rested right on the spruce pole.

"The bear goes up the pole by clawing up with his paws on each side. The pole is too narrow for him to walk up ... he evidently had his nose right on the pole.

"I used to do a lot of meat cutting. I used a bag of pig lungs, livers and guts and hung them up the pole. Boy, they got ripe after about three days.

"I got one bear the first night. I was calling a field, calling coon with the Burnham Brothers coon call in a cornfield and a bear came over ... within probably 30 yards. I had a .22 magnum and actually put the scope on him for a minute ... I thought better of it.

"So the next morning I went back to the same place. I had just butchered a pig the day before and I just took the guts and hung them on a running pole with a snare the snare loop suspended on the ground side of the gut bag. I had the bear by 3 o'clock that afternoon ... just before dark (this time it was in Alaska — editor). It got right

The runing pole (sometimes called leaning pole) set effectively finishes off nuisance bear that must be disposed of. The bear succumbs surprisingly quickly. Note that the snare loop is right down on the pole.

in the snare. He was dead in no time. He did the same thing. He came down off the running pole. The snare was missing and he went about 15 feet. I used a drag and he wound up hard on some small brush and died. Just like that.

"Their windpipe lies right on the surface. They have a round, stout neck and you can feel the windpipe on the bottom of their neck. I caught one that sat overnight and it started to spoil a little bit, in fact. Neck snares kill them so quick that you should check them twice a day because if it's warm weather, a bear will sour. The heat will stay because they are so fat and have so much hair. They'll lay on the ground, and they'll slip and sour on the part that's on the ground."

Major L. Boddicker, writing the section on bear control in *PREVENTION AND CONTROL OF WILDLIFE DAMAGE* addresses neck snares. He recommends an 18" snare loop set with the bottom about 15" off the ground. I would probably go with this larger loop diameter. A big bear can have a large head. Also, all bears have wide shoulders. As long as the loop goes over the head, the shoulders and chest will certainly stop it and force it to snug up. Only thin critters like mink and otter are tough to snare — they can slither through a snare

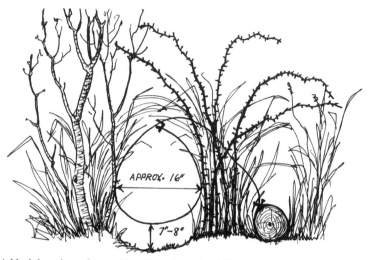

A black bear is used to pushing through brush with his head and can be easily neck snared. This neck snare is tied to a drag (end view). Note the dimensions, for even a large bear carries his head low during most of his travels. Brush or a duck stick will ensure his head is down at the critical moment. Neck snares guarantee a dead bear and are illegal in Maine for licensed trappers. They are only for nuisance bear control where relocation is not possible and a dead bear is mandatory.

loop barely larger than their head and not snug up the loop.

As for height of the loop, a lot depends upon the particular snare set. A duck stick, natural or contrived, forces a bear to drop his head right into the snare loop. In this respect, I'd rather have a slightly lower loop with a duck stick on top of the loop than to have a loop too high. On a black bear, any ground to loop bottom distance of 7" to 15" will work — as long as the bear is forced to drop his head under a duck stick.

A good point of the Major's is to keep neck snare use restricted to areas where there'll be no activity by other large animals. Neck snares are selective to a point, because of their loop size and ground-to-loop height. A bear-sized neck snare is totally harmless to man and small to medium critters. It might pose some threat to other large mammals, however. For this reason use discretion.

I am aware of two manufacturers of bear neck snares, Thompson and Gregerson.

Thompson puts out four different models: #5-XX-10', swiveled, for black bear; #6-XX-10', swiveled, for large bear including grizzly; #5-S-120", center swiveled, for black bear and timber wolf; and #6-

S-120", center swiveled, for heavy bear including grizzly. The Thompson company has been around for many, many years and is a very popular brand in Canada and Alaska.

Gregerson makes an entire line of animal snares including a #16 bear snare.

Both brands of snares are sold by a number of trapper supply houses. Check the resource chapter at the end of this book for names and addresses. At the time of this writing, the bear snares range in price from $6 to $15 each. The higher price tag naturally going to the large bear/grizzly models.

SETTING
THE FOOT-GRIPPING TRAP

Because of the negatives of danger, high price, difficulty to find (being antiques), weight, additional regulations, and likelihood of theft, steel-jawed bear traps are not recommended for bear trapping. For those that choose to go this route, use extreme caution.

To find a bear trap, you must contact trapper supply houses and study the classifieds in both *THE TRAPPER & PREDATOR CALLER* and *FUR-FISH-GAME* magazines. With some luck, you will find one to two for sale. They also sell at the larger trapper conventions by hobbyist trap collectors.

Bear traps can be concealed on bear trails (highly dangerous to others), in front of dirtholes, or in cubbies. As Art Bousquet recommends, use these traps in cubbies.

To set one of these longspring traps, clamp both springs closed with a set of trap clamps. Now open both jaws and flip the latch over the near jaw. Now raise the trap pan so the notch on its hinge side fits over the latch. Place a block of wood under the pan to keep it in the up position. This is makeshift, but serves as a lock. It is not a guarantee, but will help keep the trap from firing before it is set. Always handle the trap by the springs. Always keep clear of the jaws.

Using the trap as a guide, cut out a trap bed large enough so the trap will just snuggle in under the ground level. Place the trap so it won't rock or tip. Dig out high spots and fill in with sod where necessary. Place a pencil-sized stick in the trap bed so it sticks up next to the trap pan and latch. This is to keep the bear's paw from half stepping on the latch. Place this stick by lifting the loose jaw and **REACHING UNDER IT!** Now place stepping sticks on either side of the jaws. Make sure the sticks are far enough away so the jaws will

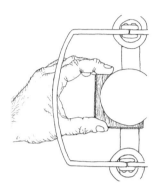

miss them when they are fired. A patch of moss that fits inside the jaws works as well here as with a foot-snare. Again work this in position by reaching under the loose jaw.

The moss in place, lift up the loose jaw, and **REACHING UNDER IT** and the moss, pull out the block of wood from under the trap pan. Carefully let the loose jaw and moss back down.

Now conceal the trap with a light covering of leaves and other woods floor debris. Don't put any covering over the moss and don't use any sticks that might wedge the jaws open if they get caught near the jaw's hinge. Sprinkle this concealment from far above the trap. Don't get those hands too close.

Place a block under a bear trap's pan so it is wedged upward. This is additional insurance against a trap firing during the setting process. Remove the block during the last stages of concealing the trap. Set the trap and work with the block only by reaching under the trap's loose jaw (the jaw not held by the trigger latch). The steel-jawed trap is not recommended for bear, and, if used, must be handled with great care.

The trap chain should be cabled to a tree or log drag as with the foot-snare. Do everything at a steel-jawed trap set, except actually setting the trap, first.

String the wires, hang the signs, place the bait, anchor the trap ... everything. The very last step is to actually set the trap. Once set, back away and don't decide to do any further doctoring of the location. To do so invites one of those situations where you hit your hand on your forehead and say *"Gee, I could have had a V-8!"* Only in this case, you'll be cussing your every fiber for having stupidly backed into your own set. You just don't ever want to make that mistake with a bear trap!

AGAIN: I DO NOT RECOMMEND USING STEEL-JAWED TRAPS FOR BEAR. THERE ARE TOO MANY BETTER ALTERNATIVES. IF YOU MUST USE THEM, EXERCISE EVERY PRECAUTION POSSIBLE TO ENSURE BOTH YOUR OWN SAFETY AND THE SAFETY OF OTHERS.

MANAGING
THE LINE

The baits have been in place for four weeks. The action at several has been intense. Bear come in daily, eating the bait and generally working it over. At some locations the bear visits have been less frequent, but still fairly steady. It's time to place the traps and run the line.

The capability to make a good set raises the bear trapper up to the next rung of the ladder to success. But, bear trapping is more than running baits and punching in sets. Further skill is required to avoid small game, to avoid small bear, to catch a bear, and to catch the bear one wants. This skill is trapline management.

Maine only allows a trapper to set two traps for bear, whether foot-snare or steel-jawed trap. With only two sets out on any one day, you want to ensure both have excellent chances of success. Too many things can happen to put them out of commission — the single bear on the bait may be spooked off or killed by a hunter somewhere else on its rounds, or small game may trip the trap before the bear makes his visit to the bait, and so on.

If you have only one really hot bait to trap, then you have a real easy call to make — set both traps at that one bait. Simple.

But if you have different baits being worked? You must begin to use your observations and gut feelings. If you have no bait that stands out as being hit every night, and at least two baits are being hit on a so-so basis, then you'll want to go with the increased odds of having one trap at each of two of these baits. This will double the odds of being in the right place at the right time.

An exception exists even for placing two traps at the hottest bait, or setting each trap at two equally good baits. Big bear are the exception. Many deer hunters pass up smaller bucks each year in hopes of a real trophy. Bear trappers, too, will ignore "sure-bet" baits to set at less certain baits with sign of a real behemoth of a bear. Trophies don't run to step into traps of any kind. Their size and desirability automatically mean they will be a bit more cagey and difficult to dupe. Even here there are exceptions, but figure that bigger bear are tougher to tag.

Once the traps are set, the sleepless nights of doubts and exhilarations stretch from dusk to dawn.

With traps in the ground, it pays not to vary your routine. The bear have become accustomed to your timing and manner of visiting the baits and rebaiting. Even if you have two traps on a single, really good bait, don't forsake the others you've been laboring over. Anything can happen, and you may wish to set up another location just days after the opener.

"I'll walk right in", says Joe Baldwin, *"and if it needs some bait I'll put it on. Normally I always have a bucket with me, a little extra pastries. Quite truthfully, in this bear trapping/bear baiting, if you've done that advance work, you won't have a problem. In a day or two, or a night or two, you'll have your bear. Or at least you'll have a hit. Now after they've hit that trap and that thing goes off, it might shy them off for a week, ten days, a month ... they might never come back.*

"You want to make it right the first time. After you do all that advance work, set that trap right the first time, so that when it springs, it's going to go and it's going to have a bear.

"The first night you go in there and a raccoon has sprung it. Try it again another night. But if you haven't done anything in a couple of nights, then you probably should be looking around for an alternative bait.

"If a trap's sprung, well, most of the time you look for tracks, scat ... you do a lot of guessing. Normally, if it's just sprung and in the ground, the weather did it or small game just tripped it. Normally, if you missed a bear, the spring will be out of the ground ... you had a hold of him for at least a minute and he just pulled out. He'll have the spring pulled off to the side and what have you. Bear don't usually spring it and it just lays in the trapbed."

Bear can become bait- and trap-shy. Such bear show greater caution. They may become wary of baits and only visit them at night. Such a bear has probably been shot at from a bait in the past. Experience has taught him that baits in daylight spell danger whereas baits at night are safe to feed upon. This bear, though almost impossible for a bait-sitting hunter to shoot, is still a practical target for the trapper. A trap-shy bear is another matter.

A trap-shy bear has become that way for one reason: He has been whacked on the nose or otherwise spooked by a trap. Maybe he had even been caught in one as a small bear and released by a trophy

Successful trappers are masters of their craft. The skill that sets them apart is trapline management. Good trapline management will enable the trapper to circumvent potential problems and latch onto the right bear.

seeker. Whatever the training, a trap-shy bear can become as cagey as an old, alpha, male coyote. A trap-shy bear requires a trapper to match wits on a much higher plane. If the bear continually steps over a trail set and simply won't step on the trigger, then try rearranging the stepping sticks. If it still doesn't work, then add a dirthole set. Just keep experimenting until you find something that the bear isn't familiar with so you can fool him.

More than a trap spring whack on the nose can put the bear off a bait. The bear get used to the fellow doing the baiting. Thirty days of baiting puts a daily dose of the trapper's or guide's odor in the area. The bear get used to it. Bring another person to the bait and it's possible to upset the bear's routine. Placing a trap in a trail, may do the same. The bear is no dummy. If he's unsure about this new factor he may take a day or two to get used to it.

It becomes a real guessing game at times to know whether to faithfully keep those traps in the ground if the bait suddenly goes cold. Is the bear just backing off a day or two to get used to the new sign at the set? Is the bear gone for weeks? Is the bear gone forever? It can frazzle nerves.

A lot of things can douse a sizzling hot bait into a granite cold pile of slop. In addition to an exceptional bear being spooked off by a second human or trap-setting activities, it's possible that a pack of coon hounds was worked through the bait area and spooked off the bear. It's also feasible that the bear visits and feeds off of other baits — baits you aren't aware of over the next hill from yours. And in this case, a suddenly cold bait may mean the bear has had an arrow shot through him or was bagged by another trapper.

Additional human activity is one of the worst things that can happen around a bait. Sometimes the bear just finds a better food source. They get tired of your meat and honey. Bruin's got a cornfield five miles down the road and he goes to that, or maybe a nice prime apple orchard. It happens. Who's to say why they do it? Bears are animals and they do as they please. At times, for no apparent reason, they move.

Regardless of the reason, a disappearing bear raises untold questions.

Whether to move traps to another bait can be the most agonizing question a trapper faces. What if the suddenly cold bait has no hits for three nights? You have four more nights of a week vacation before you must quit. Do you tough it out and hope the bear is just being fickle and will soon return? If you do not move the sets, you may be trapping for a bear that never returns. Do you start over again at a second-best bait? And if you move the traps will the first bear return that night to empty trap beds, while your traps have just held off the unsure visits of the second-best baits? These are tough questions that get tougher to answer as you get closer to your trapping deadline, whether season's end or end of your vacation.

Really hot baits will normally have more than one bear — maybe two or three. It is possible to have baits being hit by up to five or so bear. In this case, the bait might be regularly visited by a sow and cub, a couple yearlings and an old boar. It could be almost any combination of sex and age — just don't expect them to all be big monsters.

A large boar bear will kill smaller bear, even his own young. A female with a cub feed together, but other combinations rarely happen. If yearlings are feeding at a bait, they'll get real nervous before a big boar comes in. They don't hang around and rarely are found on the bait when the big boy arrives. Several bear might all be feeding on the same several baits in a particular area. You might have a big boar at one bait at 5 a.m., while a young bachelor regularly checks that bait around 11 p.m. At 5 a.m.? The bachelor feeds on another bait about two miles down the drainage. Even though a number of bear might be hitting the same bait, their timing is such that they'll not be likely to meet each other.

A hunter on stand can see the bear visiting the bait, and if he's observant and uses good judgement, sort out some sense of their size. But how about a trapper? It all begins with the baiting.

Sometimes you can find a track around the bait area. The size of the track gives a good indication of the bear's body size. Most area's won't be very suitable for leaving a readable impression — naturally. When you begin baiting, rake an area about six feet or so in diameter around the bait. Don't get it ready to plant carrot seeds, but rake up the leaves and debris so you can get a track in the dirt.

Once bear hit the bait, you can rake a section of the trail. This, too, will help you find measurable tracks.

The average black bear leaves a front foot track about 4 1/2" wide and 5" long. The larger hind foot leaves an impression 4" wide and 7" long. Use this only as a guideline. There's no substitute for the experience of observation and firsthand knowledge. Study the feet and body sizes of bear in zoos, museums and at game department check stations. Compare track sizes at various baits to determine which locations give the odds for the largest trophy.

Oh, yes, if you are a home boy looking for good eating only, then try to target the bear that field dresses under 200 pounds. Such a bear is the best for cooking. Handle and cook it as you would a hog.

A trapper or hunter can use other sign to judge bear size — and different sized sign tells you that you have a multiple-bear bait.

Scat, or dropping, size somewhat indicates bear size. It's iffy, primarily because many of the bear's foods will give the bear the diahrrea. Such sign, of course, only indicates bear. It will give no real idea of the bear's body size.

Fresh clawing on a tree should be sought. The largest bear can stretch the highest to leave their mark.

When hanging pastries up at the bait, hang them up at different heights. As with tree clawing, the higher the pastries the bear can reach, the bigger the bear.

Sometimes a bait will continue to be hit and the traps won't be touched. The bear shows extra caution with the trap, or may be a lottery winner who exhibits extreme doses of luck. Bear can become

Above: ""When hanging pastries up at the bait, hang them up at different heights ... the higher the pastries the bear can reach, the bigger the bear."

Left: A fresh pastry bag hung amongst the remains of previous bear visits.

bait- or trap-shy. It's rare, but it can happen. If the bear has had a previous bad experience with either trap or bait, then he might become very difficult to fool. Double check the set and make sure everything is tiptop when up against a bear wandering in a lucky aura.

Sweets can lead a difficult bruin to the trap. Take portions and bits of doughnuts and sweetrolls, and drop them along the bear trail. Lead them right up to and beyond the trap. This trick is one to remember and use. Pastries can also lead standoffish bear to work within range of a revolver or bow hunter.

Finally, everything clicks.

You quietly stalk down the access trail as

A good trick on the bear trapline is to lead him right over the snare with bits of pastry dropped every few feet on the trail. Drop the sweets on both sides of the set for ten to twelve feet.

so many times before. It's as packed down as a good bear trail — with a month of baiting trips and then the setting and checking. The brisk fall winds, the scudding rain clouds and the rustling of the dry, dead leaves give an inner satisfaction. Sure, you want a bear so bad you'd almost consider quitting your job to get enough time — just a little longer is all it'd take, you're certain. Reality keeps you from seriously jeopardizing your livelihood, but the daily bear run allows the luxury of those daydreams. Anticipation and daydreaming the "what-ifs" constitute the only reward for some. And for the successful majority? The tagged trophy doesn't overshadow them. The anticipation and

The author's first foot-snared bear. It was taken on the fourth night of the trip and the second night this particular bait was trapped. The bait was a hot one set up by Joe Baldwin a month earlier.

daydreams swell to more fully compliment the end success. Running the trapline — any trapline — gives one an unequaled empathy with the wild, and it fills the mind and soul. It's a lifestyle, if even of temporary residence. And it's a nice neighborhood ...

Enjoying the line, combating all the idiosyncrasies and nuances of peculiarity that Mother Nature can throw at a trapper, you make that daily, hopeful run. And there it is!

Your nostrils fill with pungent, castor-like wood smell. The low light under the spruces give the emerald moss carpet an eerie aura. Just as a clear line of vision is reached, you spot a large, black splotch at your set — a bear.

The first bear I caught got more than the average detainee. Joe Baldwin, his helper, myself, my wife, her parents and our three boys all moved in quietly to see the unique vision of a live black bear in the Maine woods. We moved in quietly — the boys had had instructions

A lot of folks around a trapped bear can make it very nervous and extremely unpredictable. For this reason the author's photo session was cut short so the bear could be disposed of before there was any undo danger. Left to right: Josh, Lance and Ben Faler pose with this average- sized Maine black bear.

carefully laid out beforehand. They understood the importance of being still and quiet and following all our instructions exactly.

Joe stood to one side with his .30-30 ready. I carefully worked on the near side of the bear with two camera bodies and flashes. I was extremely slow because the humidity and the trip back to the van to get everyone and back had my glasses fogged up too much to easily focus the lenses. I worked slowly and carefully. Everyone else was back in one spot about 15 yards from the bear. We were careful not to surround the bear and kept to one side. Also, we made sure Joe was always in a position for a clear shot.

The longer we stayed the more agitated the bear became. Joe began to get a little uneasy. I don't blame him. Rare is the guide that has such a collection of folks next to a live bear — and regardless of our experience and our waiver of responsibility, Joe's guiding license

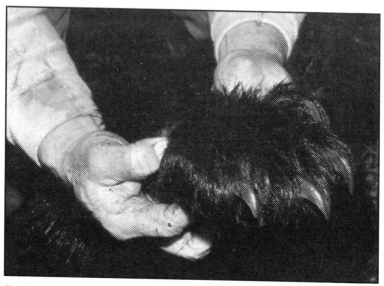

One look at a black bear's front paws and claws gives one tremendous respect for their potential. Never get too close to a trapped bear.

made him responsible for an problem that might arise. Though not at all satisfied with the few shots I had taken, I traded 35mm with telephoto lens for .22 mag with 3x scope. I leaned against a sapling for added accuracy, took my time, and centered the cranial cavity when the bear gave me a moment of no movement.

It all went smooth.

Most bear will be like that. They'll be relatively docile and tame. **DON'T LET THAT FOOL YOU! A BEAR IN A TRAP KNOWS IT IS IN A COMPROMISED SITUATION. IT HAS THE TEMPERAMENT AND POWER TO DO SERIOUS DAMAGE ... EVEN TO KILL. THE LONGER A HUMAN REMAINS CLOSE BY, THE MORE WORKED UP THE BEAR BECOMES. FINALLY IT WILL EXPLODE IN A RAGING FIT. DON'T TEMPT A TRAPPED BEAR. HE IS A FORMIDABLE FOE AND SHOULD BE DEALT WITH WITH RESPECT AND WITH ALL THE QUICKNESS AND SURENESS OF A KILLING SHOT POSSIBLE.** Take heed — these lines have been capitalized for a reason.

Almost any gun will kill a bear. Follow my recommendation, and not my example with that first bear. Use a .30 caliber. You can stand

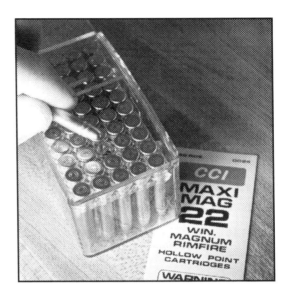

Under ideal conditions, the .22 magnum rimfire will do in a black bear. A .30 caliber is more reliable and has the stopping power necessary in case of a worst case scenario.

back and shoot the bear in the lung/heart area. This will kill any critter. It doesn't kill as instantly, stone dead as such cowboy and Rambo shots in the movies. Even heart shot whitetails, take a wild leap and run solid for 100 yards or so before dropping dead. If taking this shot, a killing shot that takes a few seconds to culminate, then stand back a little and aim carefully. If the cable would slip at the shot, you don't want a bear, dead on its feet, mauling you.

The best shot, taking a little more care in execution, is the head shot. Never aim "at the head." That's a mistake. Rather, account for the part of the head where the brain will be and the angle of the head and your shot. These factors considered, take the shot that will center the cranial cavity. If you must use a lighter caliber, miniscule .22 rimfire, then that cranial cavity shot must be shot fairly perpendicular to thinner skull bone. This assures penetration and eliminates glancing of the slug. I prefer the head-on shot right above and between the eyes. The bear needs to be looking slightly down for best results.

A perfectly broadside shot down the ear canal works well, too. The ear canal helps funnel the slug down into the brain.

All head shots with any caliber require cool handling. Gauge the bear as you prepare to aim and squeeze the trigger. Any unexpected head movement of the bear at the trigger move and you could have a flesh-wounded, crazed, murder-in-its-eyes bear on your hands.

For small bear, a jab stick, or better yet, a hypodermic gun, will temporarily put the bear to sleep so it can be safely released.

This is not the time to play Tarzan or to be comforted by a .22 rimfire pop gun.

No matter how often the baits are reconnoitered and how certain the sign there's the chance of snaring a really small bear. Any bear is a trapping trophy, but most trappers want one that'll dress in excess of 100 pounds, and really desire a 200-pounder or larger.

If the daily check reveals a small bear, one you wish to "throw back to grow bigger," it's possible to release it. The safest method for both bear and trapper is to call the local game department personnel and see if they would be kind enough to tranquilize the bear for release. I certainly cannot guarantee that they will do so, but they will often accomodate if you ask nicely. They may wish to tag the bear and add it to their management data banks.

Bear are tranquilized either by shooting them with expensive tranquilizer guns or else by using a jab stick. Jab sticks, whether commercial or contrived, are simply poles with a hypodermic needle attached to the end. Tranquilizers can be used on any-sized bear. For bigger bruins, gun delivery is best. Jab sticks aren't made long enough for comfortable jabbing of 250 and 300 pound black bear.

The law forbids more than two traps being set at any one time. And it may take, though not usually, an entire season to get a bear. Yet, it is possible to have two bear greeting you on the same check day — even on the same bait. This may be the reason for releasing a large bear.

Two bear at once is the best reason to call the authorities. They're much more likely to help out in this situation than to be releasing smaller bear for a trophy seeker.

Bear can be released by the trapper himself. This is easier with a helper and is recommended for bear no larger than 120 pounds. Get a bigger bear, and you'd best shoot and tag it, or call the authorities.

I like how Joe explains it:

"A lot of the time you can hog tie and wrestle these 80 and 90 pound bear to the ground. You want to be sure to get his mouth tied together ... and his free front paw. Don't worry too much about the back feet. They can't hurt you too bad if you stay away from them. But it's his front foot that's loose and his mouth that can hurt. Once you snug him up, you can reach over and let the cable go. It's normally a good idea to have two guys doing it.

"I wouldn't recommend trying to let a bear over 125 pounds go. But those small ones you don't have too much problem with.

"Use slip knots so you can jiggle them loose. I don't like to let them go with a rope on them. Put a slip knot in there, normally with a stick and what have you. Normally when the bear is all free, he does one of two things. He's bewildered. He just sits there and looks at you ... take an eight or nine foot stick and move him and he'll go the other way. Or just walk away from him. He's not going to come and grab you.

"... it's a good idea to have a gun ... some of these bear have a little nasty spell in them and they might try to take a hold of you."

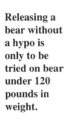

Releasing a bear without a hypo is only to be tried on bear under 120 pounds in weight.

LONG DISTANCE TRAPPING

Like my Pennsylvania friend and me, many folks interested in trapping a bruin will find it difficult to devote more than a week, or two at best, to the effort. With two solid weeks in the woods, a little homework and a lot of baiting, the odds of success are about 50/50 with a trap. This is markedly higher than a hunter sitting over his own bait. Trapping is more effective for the black bear, mostly because it's working for you 24 hours a day without the negative variables of hunter movement and scent.

If you have two weeks, consider doing the entire baiting and trapping sequence by yourself. It'll surely be an experience to treasure. Remember those one-to-one odds. To get that 50/50 chance, the two-weeker must take a lot of bait, travel many backwoods miles and, using good judgement with what he sees and with leads from the locals, place a lot of baits. You must work many baits hard in order to make contact with a bear.

While working as many baits as practical, I'd set my two foot-snares somewhere along the trapline. Until a bait was actually hit, I wouldn't necessarily set them next to one of the baits. I'd find a likely bear travelway, a grown up logging road close to and paralleling a beaver bog for example, or a likely food source, such as a ripening apple orchard, and set two dirthole sets. I would separate these to increase the odds of success.

Provided the dirtholes don't connect, I'd move them as soon as a bait was hit. Doing so takes a "well maybe" pair of sets and transforms them into "can't wait til morning, have a good chance of connecting" sets. Keep all the baits going, of course, checking and rebaiting daily. As hot baits develop, move the traps to them and let them work at least three or four nights before thinking of moving them. Variables such as a bait suddenly being hit nightly by an obviously huge bear will make you want to change trap locations regardless of the likely success where they are.

Oh, and when setting dirtholes at random until you've got a hot bait, I'd doctor them up with some long distance appeal. In addition to the bait down the dirthole, suspend a scent holder with a good douse

For the best chances of success, particularly on a week to ten-day vacation, it pays to have arranged in advance with an outfitter or guide for hot baits. Their pre-trip footwork is invaluable. *(Richard P. Smith)*

of anise over it. Draw any passing bear from as great a distance as possible.

I'd keep these sets where the normal wind direction won't be pushing all the attracting scent across a large pond. Even if a landlocked salmon would catch a whiff of it, it'll not draw much to the set. Keep this in mind when using dirtholes on two-tracks or along logging roads. Set the side of the travelway that is most likely to be the upwind side. This will usually be the northwestern side.

When after big game, a 50/50 chance is good odds. Approximately one million hunters in Pennsylvania make that annual hunt for a buck whitetail buck. The figures show that roughly 10% are successful.

For the fellow that wants the best possible chances for tagging a trapped bear, and this is especially recommended for someone with less than two weeks of time, hire a guide or rent bear baits.

There's no substitute in this bear trapping for having hot, regularly visited baits. Having a knowledgeable man on the spot who can steer you to active baits, and maybe even handpick one with a big bear on it, is invaluable. He'll take the guess work out of location and get you into some serious trapping on your first day.

Hiring a guide to take you in every day is fine. Some may prefer this to continually tap in the guide's experience. For the most part, I think this is too expensive and has a marginal increase of the success ratio compared to the increase by having a hot bait ready when you arrive.

My recommendation is to contract for two, maybe three, hot baits. Specify baits handpicked for monster bear if you wish, but these will likely cost a premium. Big bear are always in demand, and hunter or trapper will pay more for the opportunity to take one of these out of the guide's woods.

Just how much will having hot baits awaiting affect the odds? Joe Baldwin feels it increases that 50/50 ratio to an 80% to 90% comfort. Still not a guarantee, but the next best thing. Keep in mind, there are no guarantees in hunting, trapping or fishing. If a guide guarantees you'll bag this or that, you'd best look for another man to deal with. Having hunted all over the U.S.A. and Canada, and having trapping for all kinds of critters from Florida to Maine to Hawaii, I'd say that the 50% to 80-90% increase is totally accurate. If I made any adjustment to those figures I'd drop the 50% some—just because the unfamiliarity with the terrain and the technique will buffalo the efforts of some.

An out-of-state trapper can make contact with outfitters and/or guides three ways. The first is to call or write the game department. They can offer recommendations.

The second is to visit the many eastern outdoor shows so common in January and March. The one's I've attended in the Northeast and Midwest usually have a sampling of Maine guides and outfitters. Talk to them, get their rates, assess the compatability of their program with your desires. If both sides are in agreement, make a booking.

Finally, and this is my number one choice, follow Bob Noonan's advice:

"The best way to do it is to look in the MAINE SPORTSMAN. *It's a monthly and they have every bear guide known to man listed in that thing. You can get on the phone and ask these guys for credentials, what kind of success ratio, what they charge ... Be right up front with them and say, "This is what I want to do. I want to come up to snare a bear. I've only got a week, I'm only allowed two traps, and it's going to cost me $300 for the license. What would it cost me for two hot baits that you know are being worked at night or in a really tough area that can't be watched properly?"*

That "being worked at night" or "in a really tough area" can be great keys in getting any guide to rent you a bait with a big bear without too much premium being tacked on. If a bear only visits at night, the work of setting up the bait is the same, but no hunter will ever nail it. Only a trapper has a chance. And if a hot bait is in an area that is too tight, then the odds of a hunter not alarming an incoming bear are slim. Here again, the trapper excels.

Bob continues: *"I would get the* MAINE SPORTSMAN *and look for the small ads — not the big one-page ads. There's a lot of guides there that just do a few hunters. They know what they are doing. They're good.*

"My personal opinion is that the guys that do it for a hobby are really good at it and they have a very high success ratio. They might only take 12 people out, but 11 of them get bear. And there's a lot of pride in it. To them it's another way to hunt. They can only kill one themselves, but they can be in on it. You're more apt to get more personal treatment from someone like that than some big outfitter.

"If you get these small guys with the little ads, you're apt to call and find out he is working the night shift tonight, and he'll call you

back, then you're apt to spend another hour-and-a-half talking on the phone with him because he loves to do it. He'll turn you on to a good time. That'd be the way I'd do it."

I am now confident in my own bear trapping and baiting ability. With time so scarce, I'd still rent hot baits from the local boy. The minimal cost compared to travel and lodging (you can camp out) and licenses makes it a good deal.

Especially if someone else has done the prebaiting, you'll have some unused daylight after the trapping efforts. The trapping license is good for other furbearers, but their season is after bear are out. Even though you may not be able to trap other furbearers during a bear trip, a lot of small game hunting can be done for partridge (grouse), squirrels, cottontails and snowshoe rabbits. October is bowhunting month for whitetails, also. A lot of inland fishing is closed in October, but the ocean offers vast opportunities. You can go moose sight-seeing, too. The moose season is currently in September (you must be drawn, a 1:160 long-shot, and begin the process in April), but in the past the one-week season has overlapped with bear trapping seasons. Once drawn, the moose permittees have a 90-some percent success ratio. For all these, begin planning as soon as possible, and study the regulations beforehand.

Studying the regs is important. Seasons and requirements change from year to year. Wait until the last minute and you can get some real disappointments. Order foot-snares early. Make sure you have a previous trapping license from your state or a trapper training certificate from a state game department — one requirement to get a Maine trapping license. Double check dates. Complying with the regulations of bear trapping will rest squarely on your shoulders. Most guides and outfitters do not have a lot of experience with bear trapping. Their expertise is in providing a hot bait or two. Many will not have knowledge of the trapping regulations or in the details for successful trapping. The trapper, himself, provides that.

CONCLUSION

This is the toughest chapter of this book to write. I want to say I'm glad it's over and the book is completed. Good luck and maybe we'll cross paths some day. Yes, those things are true. But, I'm somewhat sad the tales of bear trapping in this work have ceased. I enjoy reliving past moments. Writing about them forces me to think ever so much more of the odors, sounds and sights of the entire experience. I'll miss the luxury of immersing myself in those past adventures.

I do have a consolation, however. Though this book is finished, the experiences continue. New adventures will unfold with time. There will be more bear and more bear tales. And, I trust, you'll grasp your share of the bear trapline.

While dumping a bucket of fresh bait at your prime location, listen to the gobby, the Canada jay, whisk by your ear and land above your head. While hollowing a foot-snare trap bed, sniff that rich aroma of the forest as it permeates the air around your digging. I wish all great success in their bear pursuit, but even more importantly, enjoy the outdoors and become in tune with it. Don't let it be a stranger.

... and maybe someday, our paths will cross.

More black bear are trapped by biologists and nuisance control agents annually than are taken by Maine sport trappers. In 1989 for example, sportsmen harvested 2150 black bear in Maine. Of these only 55 were trapped. Compare that to 240 taken by bow and arrow. *(Richard P. Smith)*

SOURCES

Maine Department of Inland Fisheries and Wildlife
284 State Street Station #41
Augusta, Maine 04333
Contact for licensing, current regulations and seasons.

THE MAINE SPORTSMAN
Box 365
Augusta, Maine 04330
Monthly newspaper with up-to-date hunting and fishing information. The best source for outfitters and guides.

Joe Baldwin
P.O. Box 15
Garland, Maine 04939
Guide and trapper

Day Fur Company
Chandler Road
Belgrade Lakes, Maine 04918
Source of foot-snares and other trapping supplies

Sterling Fur and Tool Company
11268 Frick Road
Sterling, Ohio 44276
Trapping supply dealer

M & M Fur Company
Box 15
Bridgewater, South Dakota 57319-0015
Trapping supply dealer

Three generations of the Day family of Belgrade Lakes, Maine, who run one of the largest trapping supply and fur buying operations in the state. Left to right: Gary, Mark and Jim.

World Traders, Inc.
Bar Harbor Road
Box 158
Brewer, Maine 04412
Manufacturer of Mowatt foot-snares and other trapping supplies

FUR-FISH-GAME
2878 E. Main St.
Columbus, Ohio 43209
Trapping trade advertisers

THE TRAPPER & PREDATOR CALLER
700 E. State St.
Iola, Wisconsin 54990
Trapping trade advertisers